DOVER *Pictorial Archive* SERIES

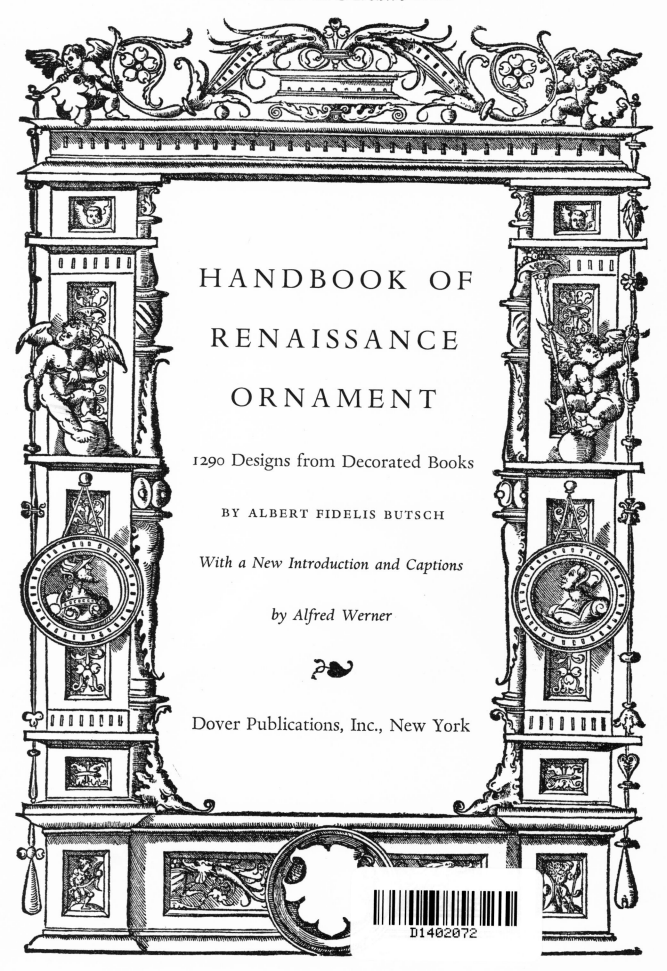

HANDBOOK OF RENAISSANCE ORNAMENT

1290 Designs from Decorated Books

BY ALBERT FIDELIS BUTSCH

With a New Introduction and Captions

by Alfred Werner

Dover Publications, Inc., New York

Copyright © 1969 by Dover Publications, Inc.
All rights reserved under Pan American and International Copyright Conventions.

Published in Canada by General Publishing Company, Ltd.
30 Lesmill Road, Don Mills, Toronto, Ontario.
Published in the United Kingdom by Constable and Company, Ltd.
10 Orange Street, London WC2.

Handbook of Renaissance Ornament, first published in 1969, contains all the pictorial material from the portfolios of Butsch's *Die Bücherornamentik der Renaissance*, originally published by G. Hirth, Leipzig, 1878 and 1880 (the second part with the separate title *Die Bücherornamentik der Hoch- und Spätrenaissance*). The present edition also includes a new Introduction written specially for Dover by Alfred Werner, as well as captions specially prepared by Dr. Werner and based on material in Butsch's text volumes. The Indexes were also drawn up expressly for the present volume.

Handbook of Renaissance Ornament belongs to the Dover Pictorial Archive Series. Up to ten illustrations from this book may be reproduced on any one project or in any single publication free and without special permission. Wherever possible include a credit line indicating the title of this book, author and publisher. Please address the publisher for permission to make more extensive use of illustrations in this book than that authorized above.
The republication of this work in whole is prohibited.

Standard Book Number: 486–21998–4

Library of Congress Catalog Card Number: 68–13685

Manufactured in the United States of America
Dover Publications, Inc.
180 Varick Street
New York, N.Y. 10014

HANDBOOK OF
RENAISSANCE
ORNAMENT

CONTENTS

INTRODUCTION

oday it takes only a few weeks to produce a book once the manuscript has reached the printer. It now requires little more time to make a million copies than a thousand; today's presses turn out about twenty million volumes daily. Easy and quick dissemination of information is, of course, a blessing, but it must be admitted that most new volumes are devoid of aesthetic appeal. One can understand the nostalgia which the British designer and engraver Walter Crane, an important figure in the Art Nouveau movement, had for the illuminated manuscripts of the past when he praised the medieval artist-scribe who "could work quietly and lovingly to make a thing of beauty with no fear of a publisher or printer before his eyes, or the demands of the world market." More recently, even Will Durant, less romantic about the Middle Ages, less inclined to ignore the sordid underside of a society in which erudition and artistic talent were concentrated in the minds and hands of a few, regretfully contemplated the artistic deterioration of the book in the post-Gutenberg era: "We paid a price for print!"

The unappealing, unattractive "commercial" book, however, did not appear right after printing with movable type had been invented in Central Europe. It took the printed book a very long time to develop the defects that were to be decried by reformers like Crane and, in particular, his more widely known associate William Morris. Unquestionably, Johannes Gutenberg's celebrated 42-line Bible—so called from the number of lines in each column—ushered in a revolution beneficial to all. The handwritten book rarely existed in more than two or three copies; prior to the mid-fifteenth century, individual ownership of books was exceptional, and even the largest universities had no more than a few hundred books in their libraries. In some of the splendid handwritten books the miniatures were far more important than the text. An abbot might allow a high-ranking, but totally illiterate, visitor to look at the magnificent illustrations serving as pictorial elucidations of the word of God Himself (most books in pre-Renaissance Europe were in the service of the Christian religion). With their colored initials, painted borders, heraldic devices and often full-page symbolic illuminations, these books were precursors, as it were, of the picture galleries that were to develop in Renaissance courts.

In the course of the fifteenth century, with the increase in the proportion of people who could read and the concomitant invention of printing, the basic function of the book illustration slowly changed. Gradually, it lost its preponderantly practical use—that of an aid in education—while retaining its purely aesthetic value. Thereupon publishers and printers—identical for a while—sought to make their products as attractive as possible to buyers who were still familiar with the old handwritten books, so as to sell their wares. Thus the early printed books were often intended to look like illuminated manuscripts, and their makers had no other thought than to reproduce the beauty of yesterday's books as cheaply and as quickly as possible. While Gutenberg himself was not particularly interested in ornamentation or illustration, most of his successors were, at times to the point of relegating the text to a secondary place. Significantly, in its first century the printed book could boast of celebrated painters in its service—Albrecht Dürer, Lucas Cranach and Hans Holbein come quickly to mind. Between *ca.* 1460 and *ca.* 1560 the world of the printed book was rich in publishers and printers with great erudition and a variety of skills, and with craftsmen who had the souls of artists.

The lowest point in quality book production was probably reached about the middle of the nineteenth century, when all courageous efforts to mass-produce books that harmoniously combined textual and pictorial elements ended in financial disaster. It was about that time that a well-to-do German bibliophile, Albert Fidelis Butsch, began to collect title pages, initials, borders, vignettes and printers' marks from books of the Renaissance age—more precisely, from the 1470's to the final years of the sixteenth century. He may have been encouraged to do so by the fact that his city, Augsburg, had been one of the most flourishing centers of book production during the Northern Renaissance. The first large illustrated book and the first illustrated Bible were printed there. Among the city's most illustrious sons was Erhard Ratdolt (1447–1527 or 1528), an eminent printer who was the first to produce a title page (see Plates 1–3). Augsburg was also the seat of Johann Schönsperger the Elder (1480–1523), Imperial court printer to Maximilian I, who employed artists of the rank of Albrecht Dürer and Hans Burgkmair.

In all likelihood Herr Butsch financed the publication of the sumptuous, impressive volumes of text and portfolios of plates that comprise *Die Bücherornamentik der Renaissance*, issued by the firm of Georg Hirth, Leipzig, in 1878 and 1880, and dedicated to Ludwig II of Bavaria (better known as the patron of Richard Wagner). On more than two hundred plates, book decorations used by printers in German, Austrian, Swiss, Italian and French cities are reproduced (chiefly in the original size) with great love and care. For each volume Butsch wrote a detailed introduction, as well as notes to the plates. We know more on the subject, modern research having scarcely begun in his time, and we have gained a clearer insight into the entire field. Hence, some of his opinions are, inevitably, no longer accepted by specialists, and certain of his attributions of ornaments to masters, celebrated or otherwise, are now questioned. Nevertheless, his texts, crammed with the information he had accumulated (largely in the vast collections of the Munich and Strasbourg libraries), have remained required reading for all interested in the subject.

Even the quickest glance through Butsch's work—the plates of which are now reissued by Dover Publications in a single volume—will immediately reveal one fact: the great majority of the samples are of German origin. This may astonish the reader, yet Butsch was motivated by anything but chauvinistic pride. He lavishes praise on the Italian printers, especially those of Venice, which, around 1500, had about two hundred presses, or approximately as many as all other Italian cities together. He admires the work done in Paris and Lyons. Yet just as Renaissance Italy had a Leonardo da Vinci, a Raphael, a Michelangelo, Gutenberg's native land was the leader in the art of printing, as well as in graphic art, which played a more important role in Germany than in any other country. Not only did the 42-line Bible originate in Mainz—it is irrefutable that Germans, rather than Italians and Frenchmen, pioneered in the creation of the printed book adorned with illustrations. Gutenberg's associate Johann Fust, and Fust's son-in-law Peter Schöffer, produced the first printed book—a Latin Psalter—to contain elaborate initials (Mainz, 1457). In the early 1460's, Albrecht Pfister of Bamberg issued the first printed book to make use of woodcut illustrations. Some of Italy's finest decorated books originated in printing shops founded by German immigrants.

In the German-speaking territories, Nuremberg, Augsburg, Ulm, Frankfurt, Strasbourg, Mainz, Cologne and Wittenberg excelled in the production of books, though printers of importance appeared even in obscure little towns. In Switzerland, Basle and Zurich must be mentioned. Basle's shining light was the printer Johann Froben (1460–1527; see Plates 42–50, 52, 56–58, 63, 67), an outstanding humanist whose chief literary adviser was the wise Erasmus of Rotterdam; among Froben's "discoveries" was young Hans Holbein, who made numerous book designs for him (see Plates 45, 46, 48, 49, 57, 58, 63). Equally important was Nuremberg's Anton Koberger (1445–1513; see Plate 39), who employed over two hundred journeymen and apprentices and had twenty-four presses going full time. Koberger's most unusual venture was the large, ambitious *Nuremberg Chronicle*, illustrated with many woodcuts by Michael Wolgemut and his stepson Wilhelm Pleyendorff. Among the other artists who worked for Koberger was his godson Albrecht Dürer.

France did not lack progressive and far-seeing publishers and printers, either. Henri Estienne (1460–1520) in Paris, and his son-in-law Simon de

Colines (see Plates 109–115), must be singled out. Estienne commissioned a Roman type, known by the name of its designer, Claude Garamond, and used to this very day. Geofroy Tory (1480–1533) was publisher, printer, designer and scholar in one person—not a rarity in the Renaissance, the age of the *uomo universale* (see Plates 104–106, 109–113, 125). Antwerp's pride was an immigrant from France, Christophe Plantin (1514–1589; see Plates 151–153), whose large and luxurious illustrated books included one of the last Books of Hours.

But more important than any of these men, and perhaps greater than any of the publishers to come after him, was an Italian—Aldus Manutius (1450–1515), of Venice—who was the first to produce inexpensive handsome books of small format for scholars. He designed many type faces, secured the services of the most prominent men of letters as editors of his compilations of classic writings, and was himself the author of the Greek–Latin dictionary he published. His edition of *Hypnerotomachia Poliphili* (Polyphilus' Strife of Love in a Dream; see Plate 8), an eroto-architectural romance in the form of a dream allegory, has been called the most beautiful woodcut book ever published (the artist's name is unrecorded, as are the names of many book illustrators of the Quattrocento, and even of the century to follow). Manutius' printer's mark was the famous Anchor and Dolphin, the anchor symbolizing the need to hold fast until the work was right; the dolphin, swiftness.

By today's standards, Manutius' Aldine Press was anything but swift. Not only the so-called incunabula—the "cradle books" printed in the second half of the fifteenth century, among which was the *Hypnerotomachia* (1499)—but even the books of the High and Late Renaissance, were produced on a crude wooden screw press run by hard manual labor which was most time-consuming (the successful application of steam power to the printing press, greatly increasing the output of the machine, dates only from the year 1810). Besides, type was not, as a rule, available in standardized letters of distinct shapes and different sizes, but for a long time was designed and cast by each printer according to his requirements and tastes.

For his Bible, Gutenberg cut a solemn, heavy type which, while of a majestic grandeur, is not easily legible. This ecclesiastic Gothic type, also known as "black letter," turned out not to be a very suitable vehicle for the vast amount of information, of new and often controversial ideas, that arose in the era of "rebirth," of Reformation and Counter-Reformation. The Humanists, in particular, felt that the obsolete Gothic type was not appropriate for the printing of the rediscovered classical authors of antiquity, nor, for that matter, for their own writings. They wanted and got, a light, clear, elegant type that became known as "Roman." Except for Germany, where the "barbaric" Gothic type, with modifications, survived into the twentieth century—it was elevated to the rank of the exclusive German national type by Hitler!—the "white letter," favored by the Humanists, became universally accepted. Much of its success is due to the efforts of the Frenchman Nicolas Jenson, who settled in Venice before 1470, and who has been called one of the greatest type designers of all time.

After vellum, or parchment, had proved uneconomical and had, except on rare special occasions, given way to paper, conscientious publishers looked for the best products of the paper mills which rose in increasing numbers all over Europe. For the embellishment of the pages, superb artists and craftsmen were often employed (though it must be admitted that frequently available cuts were used even if they did not quite fit the text). The distinction between "fine" and "applied" art was not yet made, and would, indeed, have sounded absurd. Men like Dürer, Cranach or Holbein would not have understood the modern separation of art mainly utilitarian in intention from art supposedly elevated by being of purely aesthetic significance. The fifteenth or sixteenth-century artist was glad to execute to the best of his ability any commission, including that of making initials or borders for a book.

The antique world knew only simple capitals. Initials, that is to say, letters of extra size and ornamental character to indicate the beginning of a chapter, are a product of the Middle Ages. They were carefully and lovingly drawn and painted by scribes who gave their imaginations free rein. Elaborate initials were retained in the era of the printed book, while large plain capitals came also into use (the latter were generally cast, while the more ambitious, ornamental initials were, for the most part, engraved on wood or metal).

Particularly outstanding is the Dance of Death Alphabet designed by Hans Holbein the Younger (1497/98–1543), anticipating, in theme and approach, his celebrated series of woodcuts on the same subject (see Plate 66). In keeping with the prevailing practice, Holbein left the letter, which has the classical form of old Latin script, fully intact, without ornament. But the background of the square design is filled with human figures and skeletons, to show that Death seizes everyone, from the highest to the lowest, the child in the cradle no less than the old (incidentally, Holbein's alphabet consists of twenty-four little pictures, as there was only one character for U and V, as also for I and J). Other Holbein designs are to be found on Plates 45, 46, 48, 49, 53, 57–61, 63–65, 67–69.

By the time Holbein designed these initials (ca. 1523), the embellishment of printed books had had a tradition of more than sixty years. The first illustrator known to us by name was Erhard Reuwich of Utrecht, who accompanied a nobleman, Bernhard von Breydenbach, on a pilgrimage to the Holy Land. Breydenbach's *Peregrinationes in Terram Sanctam* (Mainz, 1486) contains sketches, and even a map. Reuwich cut his own drawings into the wood blocks. Subsequently, the artists rarely bothered with this time-consuming, laborious task; it became the practice to make drawings on paper or, perhaps, on the wood block, and a special *Formschneyder* was engaged to carve the master's work into the wood. This *Formschneyder—tailleur d'image, intagliador de figure de ligno*, and, in Latin *incisor lignorum*, or simply *sculptor*—considered his own work so important that he often put his monogram on the block along with that of the designer, and even added a little figure of a knife below it. In Jost Amman's *Eygentliche Beschreybung aller Stände auf Erden* (1568), which contains over a hundred graphic representations of people in a variety of professions and trades, there is also a picture of the *Formschneyder*. Beneath is a bit of doggerel by Hans Sachs, in which the craftsman is made to boast that when the pictures are printed "you see clearly the very lines that the artist has traced, his drawing, whether it be coarse or fine, reproduced exactly line for line."

We know Holbein's *Formschneyder*, Hans Lützelburger, by name. Neither Albrecht Dürer (1471–1528) nor Lucas Cranach the Elder (1472–1553) is likely to have done the cutting himself, though, in all probability, they checked and supervised the activities of their assistants. Dürer's celebrated woodcut production, starting with the *Apocalypse* of 1498, does not really fall into the category of book illustrations, let alone ornamentations, because the texts play a rather minor role, the emphasis being exclusively on the graphic works themselves. It has not been proven that he contributed, as is generally assumed that he did, to the illustration of the *Nuremberg Chronicle.* Nor do we know with absolute certainty whether some commercial works, such as initials and marginal decorations, often attributed to him, were not actually products of his pupils (especially Hans Springinklee, who lived and worked in Dürer's house from about 1513 to 1522; see Plate 39), or even of mere imitators. He certainly did participate in the decoration of several large and lavish books, produced for Emperor Maximilian I to shed extra glory on himself and his dynasty (as the "Last Knight" was candid enough to admit). In any event, Dürer shared the experience of so many important masters who came to realize that Maecenases are often slow in discharging their financial duties to protégés. For in 1515 Dürer appealed to a friend to ask the Emperor to pay him, pointing out that "I have served His Imperial Majesty for three years, suffered loss of fortune, and had I not exerted all my industry, this beautiful work [the *Triumphal Arch*] would never have been finished in such a way." (For designs that have been attributed to Dürer, see Plates 35–38, 88–90, 125.)

Lucas Cranach the Elder also contributed a number of woodcut designs (he even owned a large printing establishment in Wittenberg, producing works in behalf of the Protestant movement). But it is very likely that most of the work in this genre often attributed to him was actually produced by two of his sons, Hans and Lucas the Younger, the former being known to have illustrated several of Luther's works, including his celebrated translation of the Bible. (For designs attributed to Cranach, see Plates 95–102.)

Though less widely known than Dürer, Cranach and Holbein, Hans Burgkmair (1473–1531), noted son of Augsburg, can be mentioned as the fourth important painter to have spent time on decorating books (he made no fewer than one hundred and thirty-seven designs for the books *Weisskunig* and *Theuerdank* and the woodcut series of the *Triumphal March*, all artistic ventures sponsored by Emperor Maximilian I). Burgkmair designs are to be found on Plates 21, 24, 27, 29–31, 33, 34. The fifth important man is Albrecht Altdorfer (1480–1538), one of the "Little Masters" (so called not because they were minor artists—which they were not!—but on account of the very small dimensions of their plates).

Of less importance, but still far from uninteresting, are several other German—or Swiss—artists of the sixteenth century who devoted much of their energy to collaboration with publishers. They are, in alphabetical order, Hans Baldung (called Grien; see Plates 73, 75, 77, 78, 80), Barthel and Hans Sebald Beham (two "Little Masters"; see Plates 154, 155, 208, 209), Urs Graf (see Plates 42–44, 107), Ambrosius Holbein (the other son of Hans Holbein the Elder; see Plates 47, 50–52, 67), Daniel Hopfer (see Plates 22, 23, 25, 26, 28, 32), Hans Leonhard Schäuffelein, Virgil Solis (see Plates 157–160, 182, 184) and Tobias Stimmer (see Plates 163, 180, 186, 197–202, 204). Gifted with rich and often bizarre fantasy, they all drew a large variety of mythological, allegorical or historic scenes, with undiminishing power of invention. They tackled religious subjects as easily as secular ones. There was nothing that they could not do—from the creation of charming alphabets to the composition of glamorous title pages, enclosed between elaborate pilasters and borders (resembling, as one writer put it, "the doorway or façade upon which the words of the title and other written parts appeared as on some ideal stage").

Their colleagues in France—among them Geofroy Tory, already mentioned, and Bernard Salomon (see Plates 133–134, 136, 138–142, 146)—were equally skilled and industrious, and often excelled the Germans in the elegance of their manner, and in what has become known as "significant form." Italy's illustrators and decorators—among them the outstanding Ugo da Carpi (*ca.* 1455–1523)—often drew their inspiration from paintings of the great masters of the *Rinascimento*. All willingly responded to the public need for information (on subjects of religion, antiquity, foreign lands and people), and, in particular, entertainment and delight.

The most industrious of all this group was the aforementioned Swiss Jost Amman (1539–1591), believed to have been a disciple of Virgil Solis. Solis was one of Nuremberg's most successful illustrators and is celebrated for two Bible editions he ornamented. In 1562, when Solis succumbed to the plague, Zurich-born Amman, now a resident of Nuremberg, took his place as the chief artist of the famous Frankfurt printer and publisher Sigmund Feyerabend (1528–1590). Amman possessed an amazing facility and fecundity. He was a virtuoso without any apparent inner drive, an artist willing to lend his unusual gifts to the requirements of supply and demand, and to furnish the kind of hedonistic entertainment that forecasts the age of the Baroque. Amman designs are to be found on Plates 161–165, 167–179, 180–183, 184–186, 203, 207.

In the above-mentioned *Eygentliche Beschreybung*—one of the scores of books carrying Amman's name—we find the printer, at a crude hand press, very much like any of the presses used in the sixteenth century (and for about two hundred years thereafter). The accompanying verses state that the art of printing originated at Moguntia, or Mainz. Indeed, the practical execution of printing is now universally credited to Gutenberg of Mainz, despite counterclaims that feebly turn up once in a while. On the other hand, the early history of the woodcut—the predominant technique used in the printed books of the Renaissance—is still obscure. Presumably it emerged almost simultaneously in both France and Germany around 1400. When Gutenberg appeared on the scene, block-books—with picture and text carved into one block—had been in existence for a number of years. Gutenberg's heirs were quick to see the advantages of the woodcut, since the wood blocks can be locked in forms with the type so that text and illustrations are printed together in a single impression. Often metal was used in lieu of wood, but this metal-cut is also a relief print, and therefore classed with the woodcut. Most printed books, far beyond the middle of the sixteenth century, used wood-cuts. The intaglio print—created by engraving or etching lines into a metal plate—was very slow to oust the older method in the field of illustration, and only in the seventeenth century, the Baroque age, did the engraving achieve a near monopoly. All examples in the present volume are either wood or metal-cuts, the vast majority being woodcuts. If a caption contains no indication to the contrary, the item illustrated is in woodcut.

One might ask: What significance, aesthetically speaking, have the decorations and ornaments offered on the following plates for our contemporary civilization? Exposed as we are daily to the austerity and even sterility of "minimal art," "primary structures," "ABC art," are we still able to appreciate the twisting, curving forms, crowded with interesting figures and shapes, that we are offered here? Are we receptive to the flights of frequently grotesque imagination, the stupendous craftsmanship often bordering on virtuosity, the exuberant love for theatrical detail mirrored in these pages?

To some of us it may appear, upon reflection, that the elimination of the human figure in general, and of recognizable objects, has impoverished the art world, and also, the craft of the book manufacturer, to such a degree that a reversal of the trend seems inevitable. Recently, though, there has been a strange re-evaluation of a phase of art in which ornament played a paramount role—Art Nouveau, also known as *Jugendstil*. In this connection, the new appreciation of the Art Nouveau books—volumes issued around 1900—with their integration of artwork and type design, their insistence on rich decorative values, their general ornateness reminiscent of late illuminated manuscripts or early printed books, is significant enough. By the same token, the hundreds of designs offered here cannot be dismissed lightly as extravaganzas or curiosities. For the masters represented here combined whim and fancy with an often high artistic conscientiousness, and some of the ornaments will carry us into that land of fantasy where man is monarch of all he surveys.

New York, 1969   ALFRED WERNER

PLATES

Plate 1. *Decorative initials from the print shop of Erhart Ratdolt, Venice, 1477. Original size.*

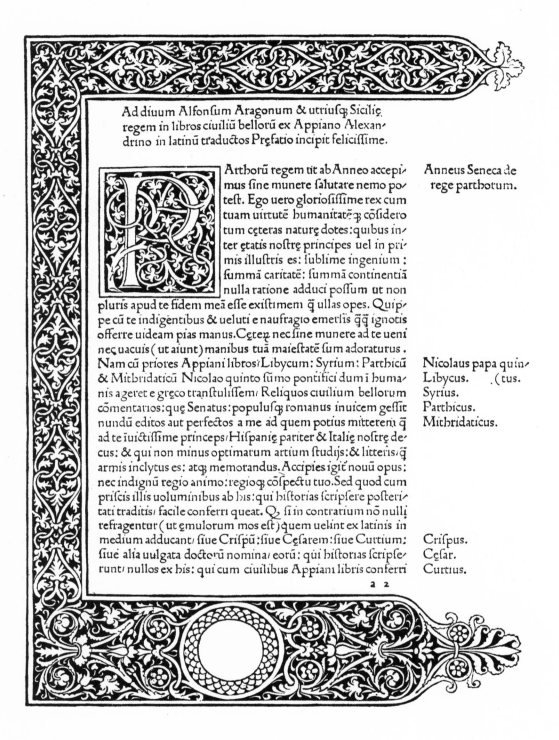

PLATE 2. *Page with initial and border decoration, from the print shop of Erhart Ratdolt, Venice, 1478.* ⅔ *original size.*

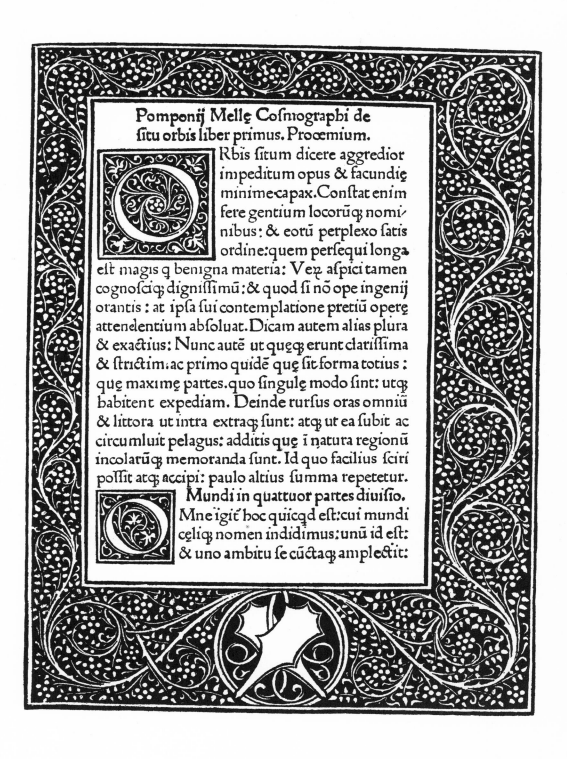

Pomponij Mellę Cofmiographi de
fitu orbis liber primus. Procemium.

Rbis fitum dicere aggredior
impeditum opus & facundię
minime capax. Conftat enim
fere gentium locorūq̃ nominibus: & eotū perplexo fatis
ordine: quem perfequi longa-
eft magis q̃ benigna materia: Veꝝ afpici tamen
cognofciq̃ digniffimū: & quod fi nō ope ingenij
orantis: at ipfa fui contemplatione pretiū operę
attendentium abfoluat. Dicam autem alias plura
& exactius: Nunc autē ut quęq̃ erunt clariffima
& ftrictim: ac primo quidē quę fit forma totius:
quę maximę partes. quo fingulę modo fint: utq̃
babitent expediam. Deinde rurfus oras omniū
& littora ut intra extraq̃ funt: atq̃ ut ea fubit ac
circumluit pelagus: additis quę ī natura regionū
incolarūq̃ memoranda funt. Id quo facilius fciri
poffit atq̃ accipi: paulo altius fumma repetetur.

Mundi in quattuor partes diuifio.
Mne igit̃ boc quicq̃d eft: cui mundi
cęliq̃ nomen indidimus: unū id eft:
& uno ambitu fe cūctaq̃ amplectit:

Prologus.

❡ INCIPIT EXPOSITIO BEATI HIERONYMI
PRAESBYTERI IN PSALTERIVM. ET PRIMO
PROLOGVS EIVSDEM.

ROXIME CVM ORIGENIS
Psalterium quod Enchiridion ille uocabat
strictis & necessariis interpraetationibus
annotatum in cõmune legeremus: simul
uterq depraehẽdimus nonnulla eum uel
perstrinxisse leuiter:uel intacta pœnitus re
liquisse:de quibus in alio opere latissime
disputauit:quo scilicet non poterat rẽ ma
gnam breui sermone concludere. Igitur
pro familiaritate quæ inter nos est:studio
se & sedule postulasti:ut quæcũq mihi di
gna memoria uidebantur signis quibus-
dam potius quã interpraetationibus ad-
notarem. Et(quod solent hi facere qui in
breui tabella terrarum & urbium situs pingunt:& latissimas regiones in
modico spatio conantur ostendere) ita in psalterii opere latissimo quasi
praeteriés aliqua perstringerẽ:ut ex paucis quæ tetigissem intelligantur
& cætera quæ ommissa sunt:quam uim habeant atq rationem . Non q
putem a me posse dici quæ ille praeterijt: sed quo ea quæ in Thomis uel
homeliis ipse disseruit uel ego digna arbitror lectione:in hunc angustũ
commentariolum referam. Psalterium græcum est:& latine organum
dicitur:quem hebrei nablath uocant . Psalmus dicitur:eo qd' a psalte-
rio nomen accepit:uel pro saltandum . Quamuis Dauid omnes psal-
mos cantasset:tamen omnes psalmi in persona christi pertinent: & qui
praetitulati esse non uidentur:apud hebreos pro uno psalmo habentur.
Nam per titulum intelligitur uniuscuiusq psalmi intellectus. Quid est
titulus nisi clauis?(Vt ita dixerim) in domo nõ igreditur nisi per clauim
ita & uniuscuiusq psalmi intellectus per clauem:hoc est per titulum in
telligitur:in cuius persona cantatur:aut in persona christi:aut in persona
ecclesiæ:aut in persona prophetæ.

aA A z

PLATE 4. *Page, with initial and border decoration (metal-cut), from the print shop
of the brothers Giovanni and Gregorio de Gregoriis, Venice, 1498. Original size.*

PLATE 5. *Decorative initials. The P and C are from the print shop of Peter Lichten-stein, Venice, 1496. The E, M, R and S are from the print shops of the brothers Bernardino and Matteo Veneti, Venice and Rome, 1492–1510. All original size.*

PLATE 6. *Various decorative initials from Venetian print shops, 1489–1500. The small alphabet with arabesques is from the shop of the brothers Veneti, the large F and H from that of Ottaviano Scoto (1489) and the large D from that of Peter Lichtenstein (1496). 95% of original size.*

Terentius cum
quinq3 comen-
tis: vz Dona-
ti: Guido-
nis: Cal-
phur.
Ascensu z Seruii.

Cum gratia: vt pa-
tet in suis priuilegijs.

PLATE 7. *Ornamented title page from the print shop of Lazarus Soardi, Venice, 1499.*
Original 285 × 188 mm.

PLATE 8. *Ornaments and initials from the* Hypnerotomachia Poliphili, *issued by Aldus Manutius (Romanus), Venice, 1499. ¾ original size.*

PLATE 9. *Decorated page from the print shop of Gregorius de Rusconibus, Venice, 1506. Original 266 × 183 mm.*

PLATE 10. *Title page from the print shop of Giovanni Tacuino (da Tridino), Venice, 1509. Original 266 × 199 mm.*

PLATE. 11. *Initials from the print shops of Ottaviano Scoto and (later) Giovanni Tacuino, Venice, 1490–1510. Original size.*

PLATE 12. *Initials from the print shops of Ottaviano Scoto and (later) Giovanni Tacuino, Venice, 1490–1510. Original size.*

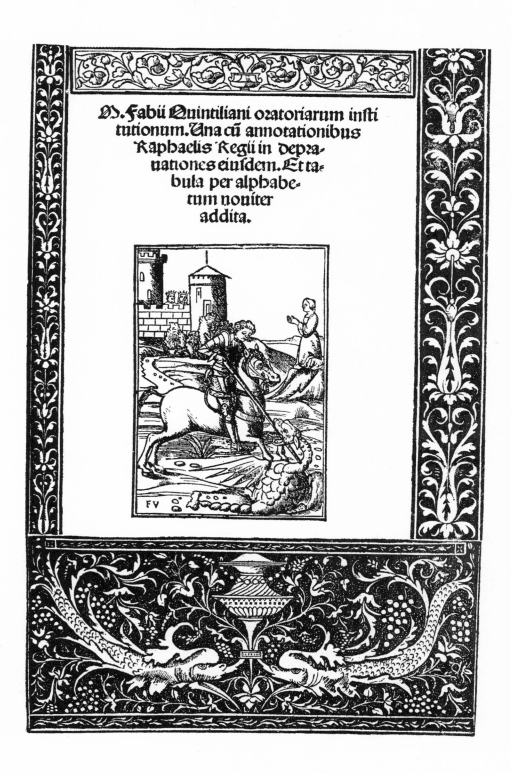

PLATE 13. *Decorated title (with St. George and the dragon), in metal-cut, from the print shop of Gregorius de Rusconibus, Venice, 1512. Original 274 × 172 mm.*

¶ Secūda pars operis dñicæ paſſionis & reſurrectionis diē ídagat, & iudæo℞ ſup hoc argumēta confutat.

Tſi multa ſunt argumenta,
quibus iudæi magnám no
bis calumniā ſolent aſtrue
re,& fidem ſperatæ a nobis
reſurrectionis ſtulta garrulitate deridere,in hac tamē
lucubratiuncula·noſtra ea
duntaxat confutare aggrediemur,quæ dominicæ paſ
ſionis & reſurrectionis materiam concernunt.Solet
nanq̃ obſtinatum illud, & ſeruile iudæorum pecus
in Chriſti ſaluatoris blaſphemiam exire propenſius
& in chriſtianorum calumniam inſultare audentius
& confidentius, quia legis noſtræ munimenta non
pauca ex auita ipſorum religione mutuati ſumus
ea præcipue,quæ agni paſchalis typo,domini paſſio
nem ſignificabant:quo fit ut perperam interpretan
tes legem,& diuini ſacra menti myſterium contami
nantes,multas indies calumnias nobis inferre nō de
ſiſtant,nunquam cauillandi finem facientes:adeo qp
cōtinuis ſubſānationibus nos laceſſentes, & ſingulas
obſeruationes noſtras deteſtátes perpetuis ipſo℞ cōtumeliis,atq̃ conuitiis ſimus obnoxii:non ſolum in
paſchæ celebratione obſeruatiōe noſtram ludibrio
maximoq̃ opprobrio ducentes(de quo ſuperiori lu
cubratiuncula noſtra ſcripſimus)uerū etiam i dñicæ
paſſionis myſterio ruditatis,& iſcitiæ nos iſimulātes

A· ii

PLATE 14. *Page, with initial and decorated border, in metal-cut, from the print shop of Ottaviano dei Petrucci, Fossombrone, 1513. Original size.*

PLATE 15. *Initials from the print shop of Ottaviano dei Petrucci, Fossombrone, 1513.*
Original size.

PLATE 16. *Page, with decorative frame and portrait of Bernardino Corio (author of the* Chronicle of Milan, *the book containing this page), from the print shop of Alessandro Minutiano, Milan, 1503. Original size 284 × 159 mm.*

PLATE 17. *Page, with decorative border, by Florio Vavassore, from the print shop of Hieronymus Soncinus, Fano (Italy), 1507. Original size.*

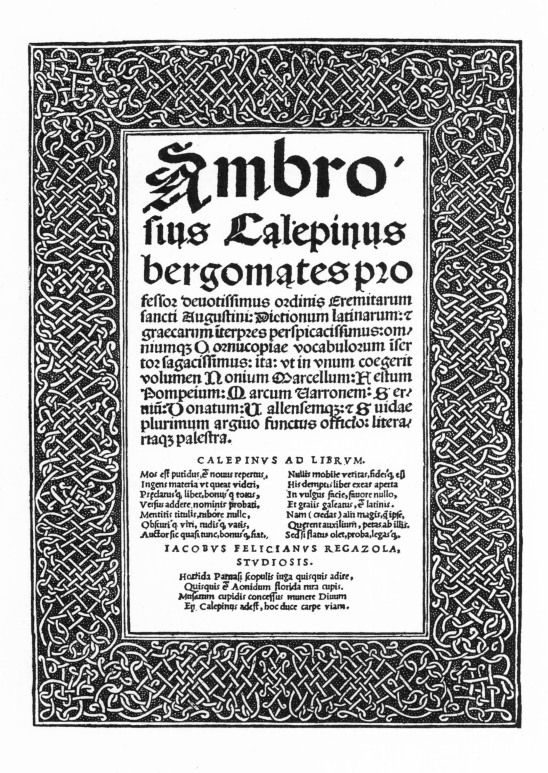

PLATE 18. *Page, with decorative border, in metal-cut, from the print shop of Alessandro Paganini, Toscolano, Lake Garda, ca. 1520. ¾ original size.*

PLATE 19. *Decorative initials from the print shop of Alessandro Paganini, Toscolano.*
¾ *original size.*

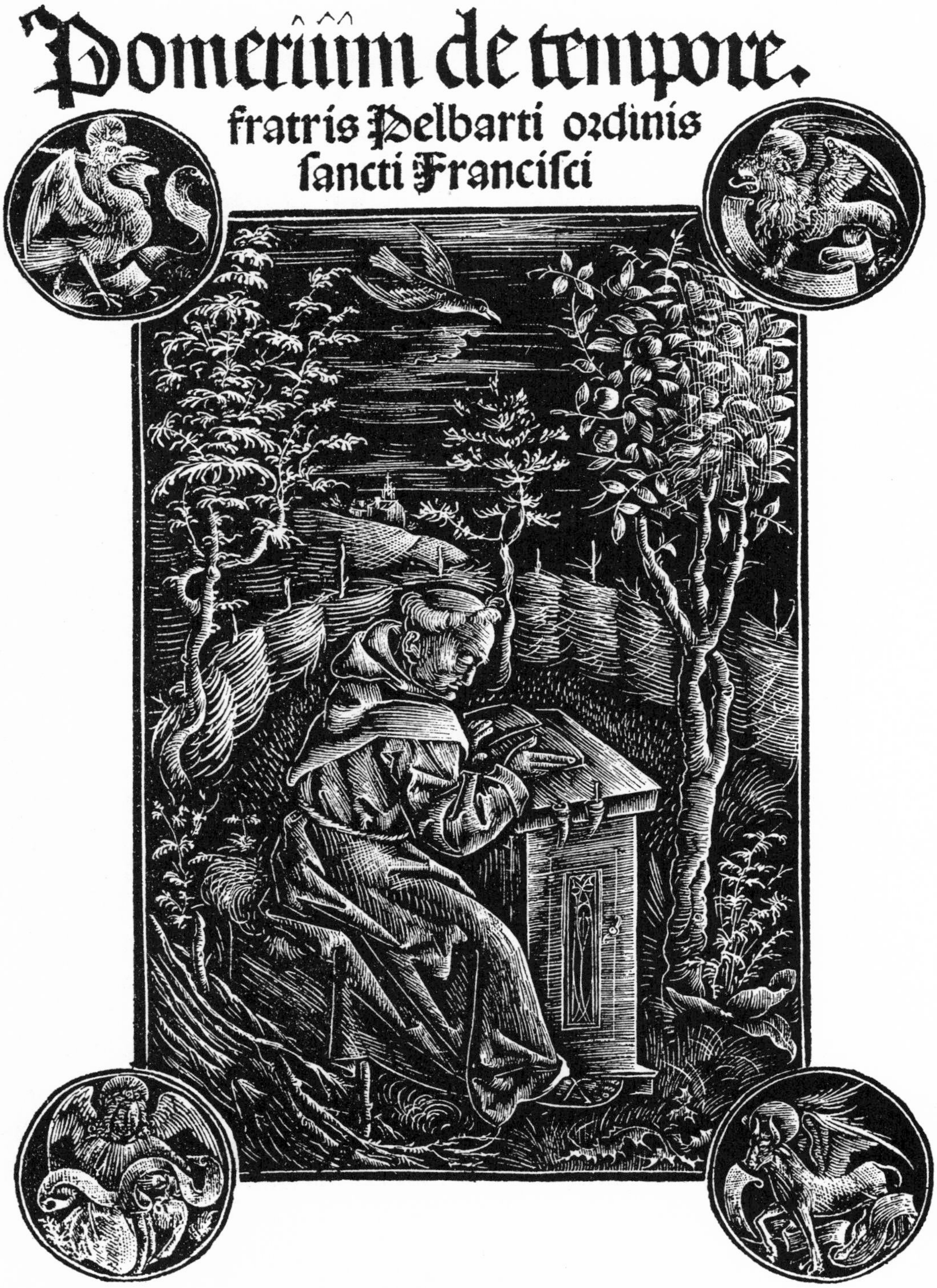
Pomeriũm de tempore.
fratris Pelbarti ordinis
sancti Francisci

Plate 20. *Title page from the print shop of Johann Othmar, Augsburg, 1502. Original size.*

PLATE 21. *Title page by Hans Burgkmair, from the print shop of Erhart Öglin and Jörg Nadler, Augsburg, 1508. Original size.*

PLATE 22. *Title page by Daniel Hopfer, from the print shop of Johann Miller, Augsburg, 1512. Original 253 × 173 mm.*

PLATE 23. *Title page by Daniel Hopfer, from the print shop of Johann Miller, Augsburg, 1516. Original 250 × 165 mm.*

IORNAN //
DES DE REBVS
GOTHORVM.PAV
LVS.DIACONVS
FOROIVLIEN:
SIS DE GESTIS
LANGOBARDO:
RVM

ALBVVINVS·
·REX·

ATHANARICVS·
·REX·

PLATE 24. *Title page by Hans Burgkmair (the* Formschneyder *was Jost Dienecker),
from the print shop of Johann Miller, Augsburg, 1516. Original 252 × 166 mm.*

Saſſenſpegel
mit velen nyen Addi-
cien ſan dem Le-
enrechte vnde
Richtſtige.

Ad lectorem Saphicum
cum Gliconico,
Saxonum dicor ſpeculum, legenti
Leges, iuracp tribuo;
Saxonum lingua loquor, ipſe Saxo
Per me iura leget ſua,

PLATE 25. *Title page by Daniel Hopfer, from the print shop of Sylvan Othmar, Augs-burg, 1516. Original size.*

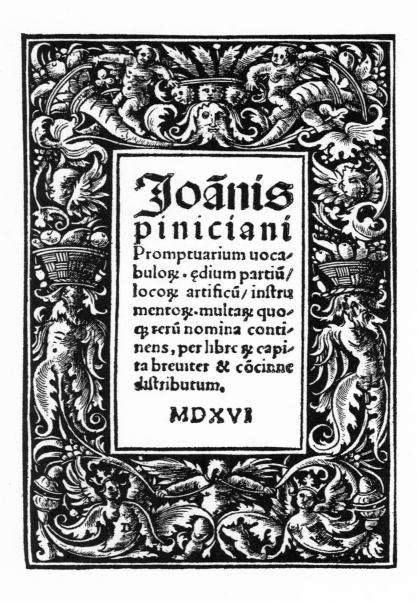

PLATE 26. *Title page by Daniel Hopfer, from the print shop of Sylvan Othmar, Augsburg, 1516. Original size.*

PLATE 27. *Imperial Eagle by Hans Burgkmair, for a title page. From the print shop of Johann Miller, Augsburg, 1516. The three large coats-of-arms are those of Ingolstadt, Freiburg and Tübingen; the date in each case is that of the founding of the university in that city. Original size.*

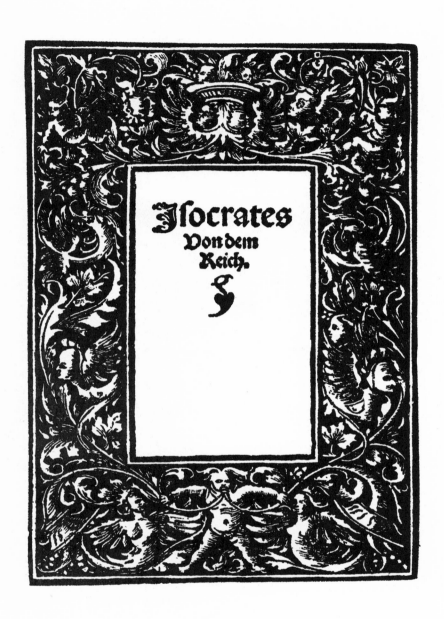

PLATE 28. *Decorative border attributed to Daniel Hopfer, from the print shop of Sylvan Othmar, Augsburg, 1517. Original size.*

PAVLI
RICII DE ANI.
ma Cœli Com
pendium.

PLATE 29. *Title page attributed to Hans Burgkmair, from the print shop of Sigmund Grimm and Marx Wirsung, Augsburg, 1519. Original size.*

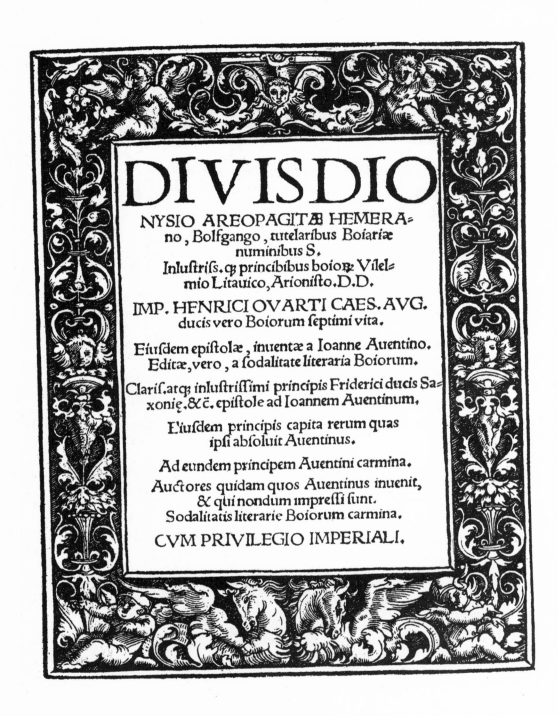

DIVISDIO

NYSIO AREOPAGITÆ HEMERA=
no, Bolfgango, tutelaribus Boiariæ
numinibus S.
Inluftriſſ. cp principibus boiog Vilel=
mio Litauico, Arionifto. D.D.

IMP. HENRICI QVARTI CAES. AVG.
ducis vero Boiorum feptimi vita.

Eiufdem epiftolæ, inuentæ a Ioanne Auentino.
Editæ, vero, a fodalitate literaria Boiorum.

Clariſ. atc inluſtriſſimi principis Friderici ducis Sa=
xoniε. & c. epiſtole ad Ioannem Auentinum.

Eiufdem principis capita rerum quas
ipfi abfoluit Auentinus.

Ad eundem principem Auentini carmina.

Auctores quidam quos Auentinus inuenit,
& qui nondum impreſſi funt.
Sodalitatis literarie Boiorum carmina.

CVM PRIVILEGIO IMPERIALI.

PLATE 30. *Title page by Hans Burgkmair, from the print shop of Sigmund Grimm
and Marx Wirsung, Augsburg, 1518. Original size.*

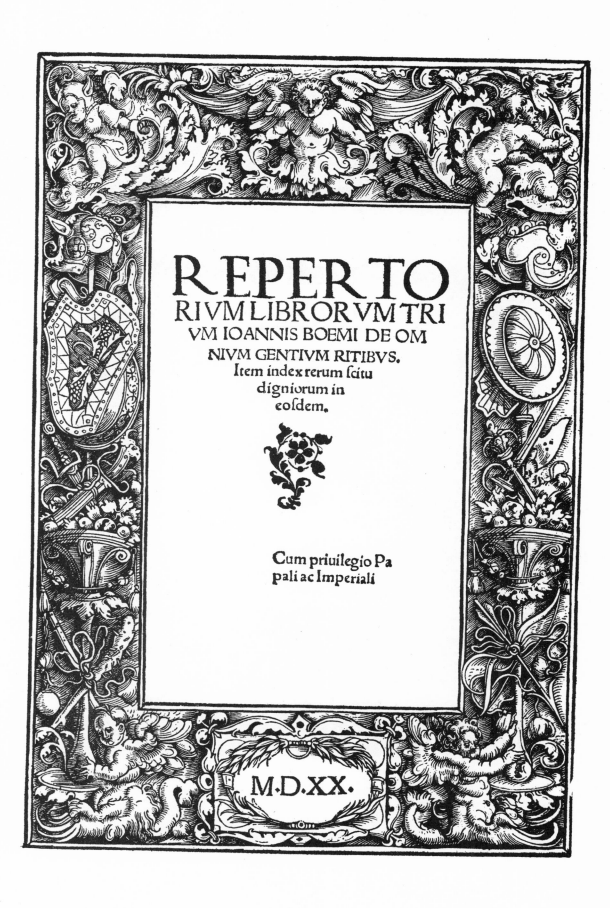

REPER TO
RIVM LIBRORVM TRI
VM IOANNIS BOEMI DE OM
NIVM GENTIVM RITIBVS.
Item index rerum scitu
digniorum in
eosdem.

Cum priuilegio Pa
pali ac Imperiali

M·D·XX.

PLATE 31. *Title page by Hans Burgkmair, from the print shop of Sigmund Grimm and Marx Wirsung, Augsburg, 1520. Original 250 × 165 mm.*

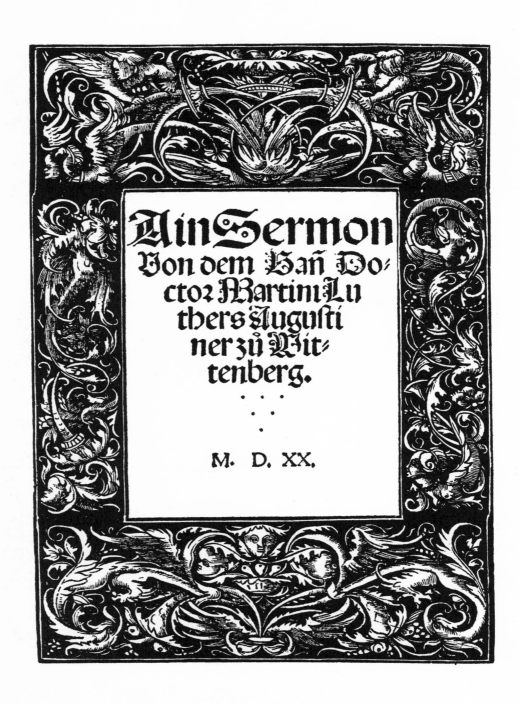

PLATE 32. *Title page by Daniel Hopfer, from the print shop of Sylvan Othmar, Augsburg, 1520. The book is a sermon by Luther. Original size.*

PLATE 33. *Initials and ornaments by Hans Burgkmair, from the print shop of Heinrich Steyner, Augsburg, 1524–1546. ⅔ original size.*

PLATE 34. *Initials and ornaments by Hans Burgkmair, from the print shop of Heinrich Steyner, Augsburg, 1524–1546. ⅔ original size.*

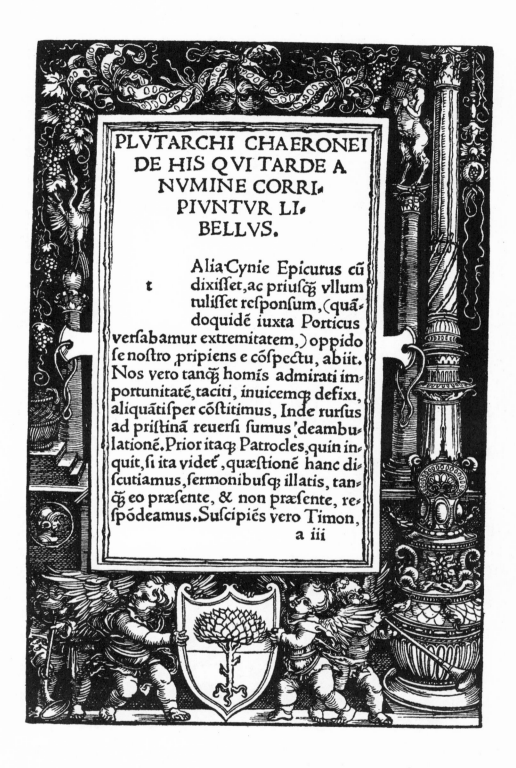

PLVTARCHI CHAERONEI DE HIS QVI TARDE A NVMINE CORRI· PIVNTVR LI· BELLVS.

Alia·Cynie Epicurus cũ dixisset, ac priusᴄ̃ᴣ vllum tulisset responsum, (quã· doquidé iuxta Porticus versabamur extremitatem,) oppido se nostro pripiens e cóspectu, abiit. Nos vero tanᴄ̃ᴣ homís admirati im· portunitaté, taciti, inuicemᴄ̃ᴣ defixi, aliquãtisper cóstitimus, Inde rursus ad pristinã reuersi sumus 'deambu· latioñé.Prior itaᴄ̃ᴣ Patrocles,quin in· quit,si ita videᵗ,quæstioñé hanc di· scutiamus,sermonibusᴄ̃ᴣ illatis, tan· ᴄ̃ᴣ eo præsente, & non præsente, re· spódeamus.Suscipiés vero Timon,

a iii

PLATE 35. *Page decorated by Albrecht Dürer, from the print shop of Friedrich Pey-pus, Nuremberg, 1513. The coat-of-arms is that of the scholar Willibald Pirk-heimer. Original size.*

PLATE 36. *Crucifix, with allegorical border, by Albrecht Dürer, from the print shop of Hieronymus Hölzel (later Friedrich Peypus), Nuremberg. 1517.* ¾ *original size.*

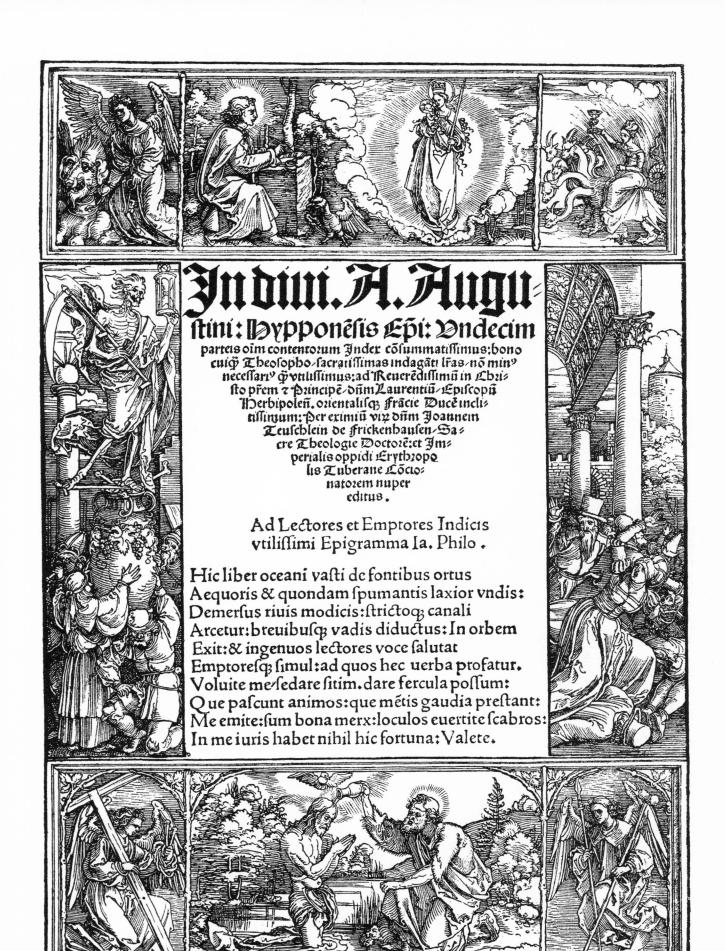

In diui. A. Augu
stini: Hypponēsis Epi: Undecim

parteis oim contentoꝛum Index cōsummatissimus: bono
cuiꝗ Theosopho, sacratissimas indagāti lꝼas, nō min⁹
necessariꝰ ꝗ vtilissimus: ad Reuerēdissimū in Chꝛi-
sto pꝛem ꜷ Principē dñm Laurentiū Episcopū
Herbipoleñ, orientalisꝗ ꝼrācie Ducē incli-
tissimum: Per eximiū viꝛ dñm Joannem
Teuschlein de ꝼrickenhausen, Sa-
cre Theologie Doctoꝛē: et Im-
perialis oppidi Erythꝛopo
lis Tuberane Cōcio-
natoꝛem nuper
editus.

Ad Lectores et Emptores Indicis
vtilissimi Epigramma Ia. Philo.

Hic liber oceani vasti de fontibus ortus
Aequoris & quondam spumantis laxior vndis:
Demersus riuis modicis: strictoꝗ canali
Arcetur: breuibusꝗ vadis diductus: In orbem
Exit: & ingenuos lectores voce salutat
Emptoresꝗ simul: ad quos hec uerba profatur.
Voluite me sedare sitim. dare fercula possum:
Que pascunt animos: que metis gaudia prestant:
Me emite: sum bona merx: loculos euertite scabros:
In me iuris habet nihil hic fortuna: Valete.

PLATE 37. *Title page, with decorations, by Albrecht Dürer, from the print shop of
Johann Stüchs, Nuremberg, 1517. Original size.*

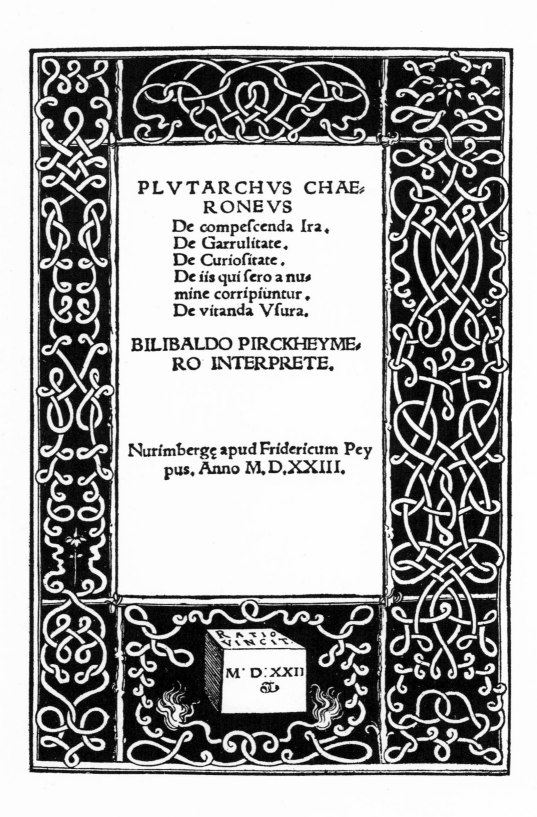

PLATE 38. *Title page, with decorations, by Albrecht Dürer, from the print shop of Friedrich Peypus, Nuremberg, 1523. Original size.*

PLATE 39. *Title page, with decorations, by Hans Springinklee, from the print shop of Anton Koberger, Nuremberg, 1516. Original 272 × 184 mm.*

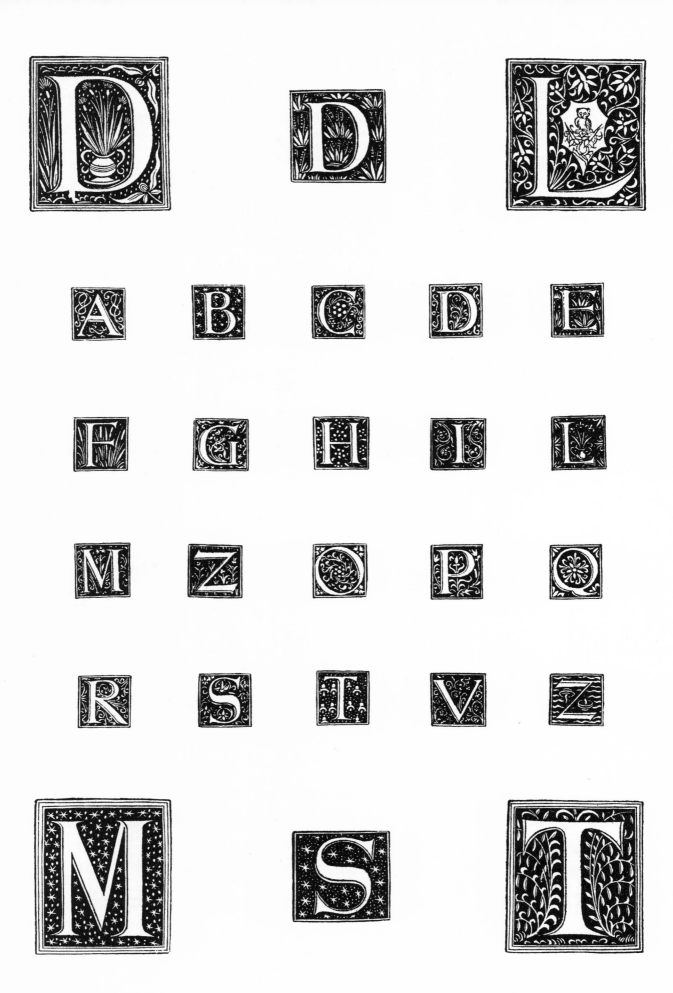

PLATE 40. *Initials from the print shop of town clerk Jakob Köbel, Oppenheim (Germany), 1512–1513. ⅔ original size.*

PLATE 41. *Initials from the print shop of town clerk Jakob Köbel, Oppenheim, 1512–1513.* ⅔ *original size.*

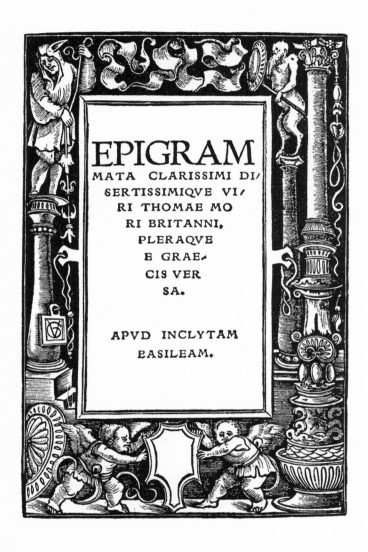

EPIGRAM
MATA CLARISSIMI DI,
SERTISSIMIQVE VI,
RI THOMAE MO
RI BRITANNI,
PLERAQVE
E GRAE,
CIS VER
SA.

APVD INCLYTAM

BASILEAM.

PLATE 42. *Title page, with border decorations, by Urs Graf, from the print shop of Johann Froben, Basle, ca. 1515. Original size.*

PLATE 43. *Decorative borders by Urs Graf, from the print shop of Johann Froben,*
Basle, ca. 1515. Originals 269 × 36 and 269 × 28 mm.

AMPLISSIMO PATRI D. THOMAE RVTHALLO EPI
SCOPO DVNELMENSI SERENISSIMI BRITAN
NIAE REGIS SECRETARIO MAGNO
ERASMVS ROTERODAMVS S.D.

MIRE VIDETVR euenisse, Præsul ornatissime, ut utriq̃ d uerso q̃
dem genere, sed tamen haud ita dissimilem militiam eodem tēpo
re militauerimus. Etenim dum tu primū regis uere inuictissimi fe
licibus auspicijs Gallos in fugam agis, deinde a castris in castra re
uersus, Scotorų regem, maximis & instructissimis copijs, in ditiōis tuæ fines
irrumpentem repellis, fundis, conscindis, ego duos omnium optimos, sed om
nium deprauatissimos autores, Diuum Hieronymū, & Senecam, a mendis, te
terrimis uidelicet litterarum hostibus, quibus hactenus nō cōtaminati fuerāt,
sed prorsus extincti, summo studio uindicaui. Et mihi cū geminis hostibus fuit
res, Nec usq̃ arbitror in uestris castris plus fuisse difficultatis, aut sudoris, q̃ mi
hi fuerit in hoc negocio. Quanq̃ hoc etiam uinco nomine, quod ũnus ipc dux
pariter ac miles, cum tot hostium milibus conserui manum, Iam nec strages in
hoc conflictu minor, q̃ in uestris prælijs. Nam aduersus Gallos, quo minus cru
enta fuerit pugna, ciuilitas hostium (nam quo potius appellē nominec) in cau/
sa fuit, qui sic ad primum statim congressum, cessere melioribus, ut appareret
in hoc ipsum uenisse, quo uobis prædam adducerent. Cæterum e Scotis ingēs
quidem contigit uictoria, nimirum ipso rege cum innumeris optimatibus cæ/
so, & eo rege, qui gladiatorio (quod aiunt) animo, summam perniciem uniuersæ
Britanniæ moliretur. Verum ea cōtigit multo uestratium empta sanguine. At
ego unico conflictu, supra quatuor hostium, imo portentorum, milia, iugulaui,
cōfodi, deleui. Tot enim, opinor, mēdas, uel ex uno Seneca sustuli. Adde quod
Scotus miles uix primos Britannicæ ditionis fines fuerat ingressus, & unicam
duntaxat occuparat arcem, unde mox depulsus est. At totum Hieronymū, to/
tumq̃ Senecam, multis iam sæculis infinitus mendarum numerus occuparat,
ut nihil usq̃ esset reliquum, quod non ab hostibus teneretur. Atq̃ hac quidē in
re mihi pro gladio calamus fuit, pro Marte Musæ, pro copijs ingenium. Nec ul
lum alioqui auxilium, in tantis rerum difficultatibus, præter duos uetustos codi
ces, quorum alterum exhibuit e sua bibliotheca, summus ille meorum studiorū
Mœcenas, & incōparabile nostri sæculi decus, Gulielmus Archiepiscopus Can
tuariensis, alterum, regium apud Cantabrigienseis collegium suppetias misit.
Sed utrunq̃ primum mutilum, deinde uulgatis etiam exemplaribus mendosi/
orem, ut minus fidendum fuerit auxiliaribus copijs, q̃ ipsis hostibus. Illud ta
men profuit, quod nō consentiebant errata, id, quod accidere necesse est in his
libris, qui ex eodem exemplari formulis excudūtur. Proinde quemadmodum
aliquoties fit, ut peritus & attentus iudex, e multorum testium oratione, quorū
nemo tamen uerum dicat, rem colligat, ita nos e diuersis mendis ueram conie/

a 2

IOANNES
FROBENI
VS SVIS
TYPIS
EXCV
DE·
BAT

PLATE 44. *Title page by Urs Graf, from the print shop of Johann Froben, Basle, 1515.*
Original 270 × 198 mm.

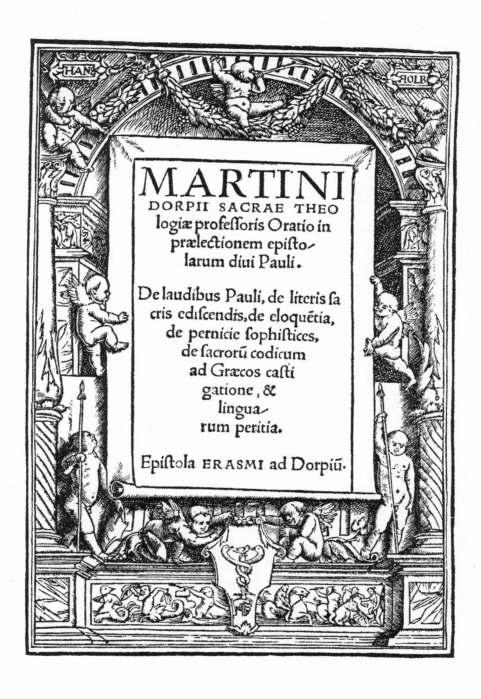

PLATE 45. *Title page by Hans Holbein the Younger, from the print shop of Johann Froben, Basle, 1516. Original size.*

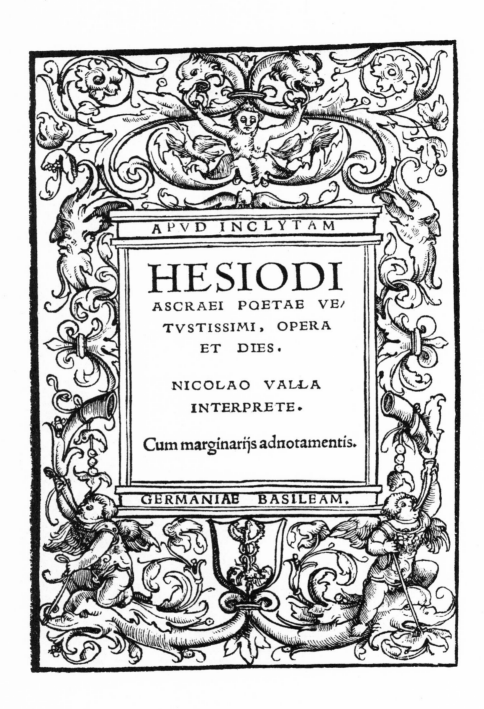

APVD INCLYTAM

HESIODI

ASCRAEI POETAE VE/
TVSTISSIMI, OPERA
ET DIES.

NICOLAO VALLA
INTERPRETE.

Cum marginarijs adnotamentis.

GERMANIAE BASILEAM.

PLATE 46. *Title page by Hans Holbein the Younger, from the print shop of Johann Froben, Basle, 1518. Original size.*

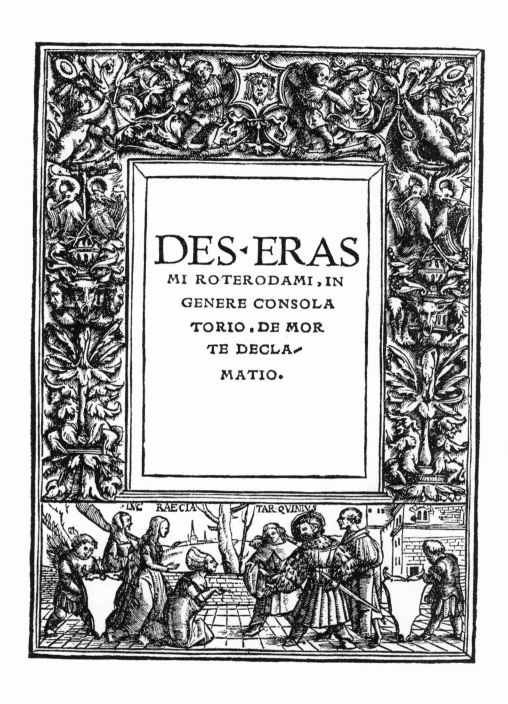

PLATE 47. *Title page (with death of Lucretia) by Ambrosius Holbein, from the print shop of Johann Froben, Basle, 1518. Original size.*

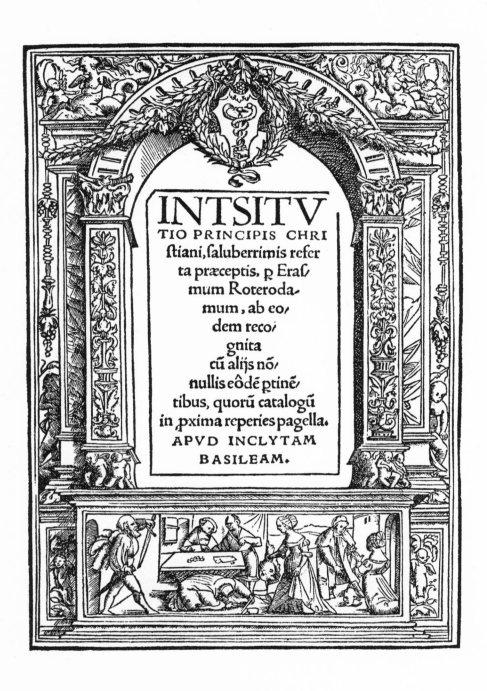

INTSITV
TIO PRINCIPIS CHRI
stiani, saluberrimis refer
ta præceptis, ꝑ Eras
mum Roteroda
mum, ab eo,
dem reco,
gnita
cũ alijs nõ,
nullis eôdé ptiné,
tibus, quorũ catalogũ
in ꝓxima reperies pagella.
APVD INCLYTAM
BASILEAM.

PLATE 48. *Title page (with death of St. John the Baptist) by Hans Holbein the Younger, from the print shop of Johann Froben, Basle, 1518. Original size.*

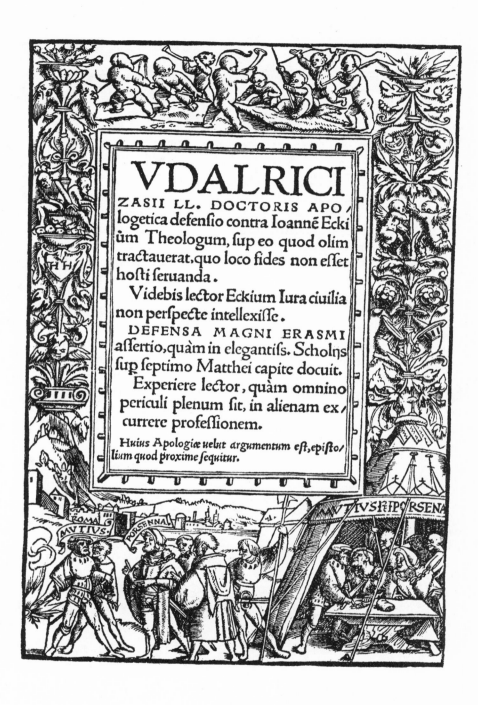

PLATE 49. *Title page (with Mucius Scaevola and Lars Porsenna) by Hans Holbein the Younger, from the print shop of Johann Froben, Basle, 1519. Original size.*

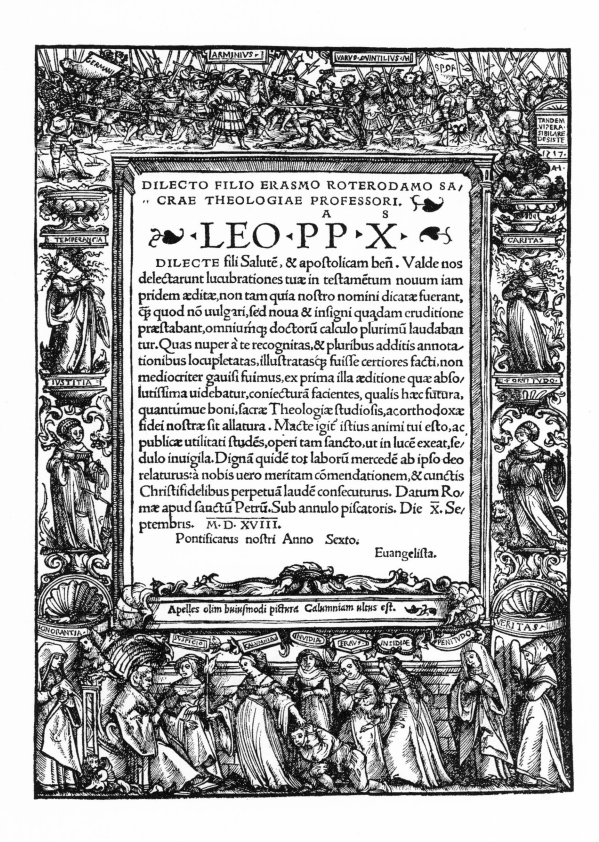

PLATE 50. *Title page (with virtues and vices, the Calumny of Apelles and the victory of Arminius) by Ambrosius Holbein, from the print shop of Johann Froben, Basle, 1519. Original size.*

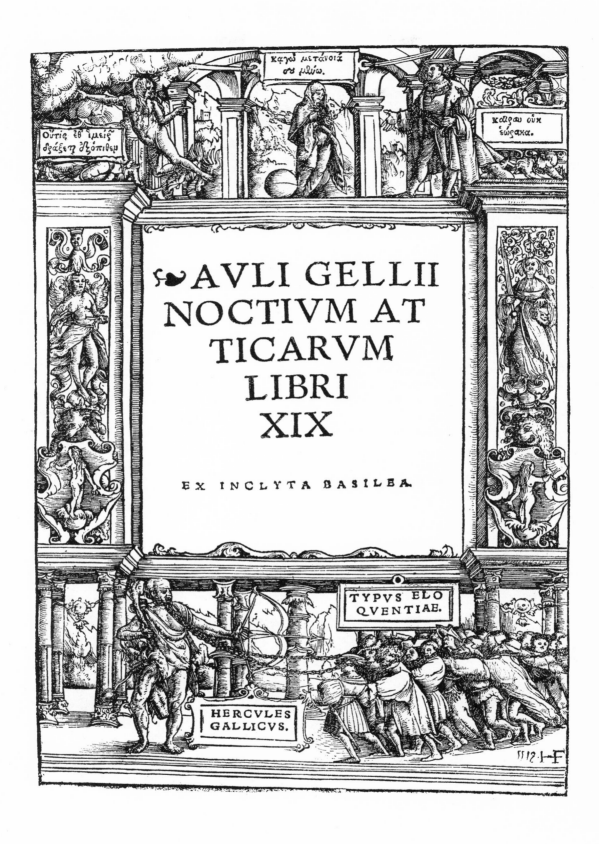

PLATE 51. *Title page (with Hercules Gallicus, an allegory of eloquence) by Ambrosius Holbein, from the print shop of Andreas Cratander, Basle, 1519. Original 265 × 178 mm.*

PLATE 52. *Page, with decorated borders (virtues, vices, courtly life, mythological scenes) by Ambrosius Holbein, from the print shop of Johann Froben, Basle, 1519. Original size.*

PLATE 53. *Decorative border by Hans Holbein the Younger, from the print shop of Valentin Curio, Basle, 1523.* $\frac{2}{3}$ *original size. The two long borders with satyrs playing instruments are by Oronce Fine, in the manner of Holbein, and appeared in a Parisian book of 1532; they are original size.*

PLATE 54. *Various colophons and printer's marks, Basle and Zurich, 1520's.*

PLATE 55. *Various colophons and printer's marks and a title page, Basle and Augsburg, 1520's.*

ᴺ REVERENDISSI

MO IN CHRISTO PATRI, PRINCIPI, AC
DOMINO D. STANISLAO TVRZO EPI‑
SCOPO OLOMVTZENSI &c. DIGNISSI
MO, BEATVS RHENANVS SELET‑
STADIENSIS, S. D.

VM in hoc uere aureo renascen
tiū literarum seculo, STANIS‑
LAE præsul eximie, quo nō mo
do tres illustres linguæ passim
discuntur, sed & quanto quæq̃
scripta sunt meliora, tanto plu‑
ris fiunt, ab omnibus operam
dari uideam, ut optimis studijs
quisque pro uirili sua consulat, Et alius quidem incognita
adhuc. Latinis auribus è Græco uertit, alius indocte uel
perperam uersa castigat aut elimat, Alius Latinos auto
res iniuria temporū deprauatos ueterum collatione ex‑
emplarium restituit, aut obscuros explicat, Ego sanè ne
prorsus sim asymbolus, operæprecium putaui, si Tertul‑
liani lucubrationes in publicum emitterem autoris non
minus uetusti quàm insignis, quibus iam per tot secula
studiosi sacrarū literarum caruerunt. Atque cum dispice‑
rem cui nam tam præclara monimenta consecrari debe‑
rent, in primis tu dignus mihi uisus es, cui scriptor anti ‑
quissimus tanquam optimo patrono dicaretur. Nam ea
es eruditione & optimarū disciplinarū peritia præditus,
& ijs perspicacissimi ingenij dotibus polles, eáque uitæ
sanctimonia cōmendaris, ut autor eruditissimus, acutis‑
simus, feruensque Christianæ pietatis assertor, libenter in
sinum tuum conuolet, nimirum ut ipsum aduersus mo
rosos quosdā qui perinde ueteribus ac nouis offendun‑
tur, tuo patrocinio defendas. Nec uero patitur epistola‑
a 2 ris angustia

PLATE 56. *Page, with decorations, by Master I. F. (or J. F.), from the print shop of
Johann Froben, Basle, 1521. Original size.*

IO. FROBENIVS PIO
LECTORI S. D.

DIVI Hilarij Pictauorũ epi
scópi lucubrationes per Erasmũ
Roterodamum nõ mediocribus
sudoribus emendatas, formulis
nostris, operacῷ nostra, quantum
licuit, ornauimus. Priorẽ æditio ›
nem nõ damnamus, sed quid in ›
tersit, ipse cognosces ex collatio ›
ne, lector optime, simulcῷ uale ›
bis. Catalogum reperies in proxi
ma pagella.

In officinã Frobeniana apud
inclytam Basileam, Anno. M.D.
XXIII. mense Febr.

CLEOPATRA

DIONYSIVS

PLATE 57. *Title page (with Cleopatra and the plundering of the temple by the tyrant Dionysius) by Hans Holbein the Younger, from the print shop of Johann Froben, Basle, 1523. Original size.*

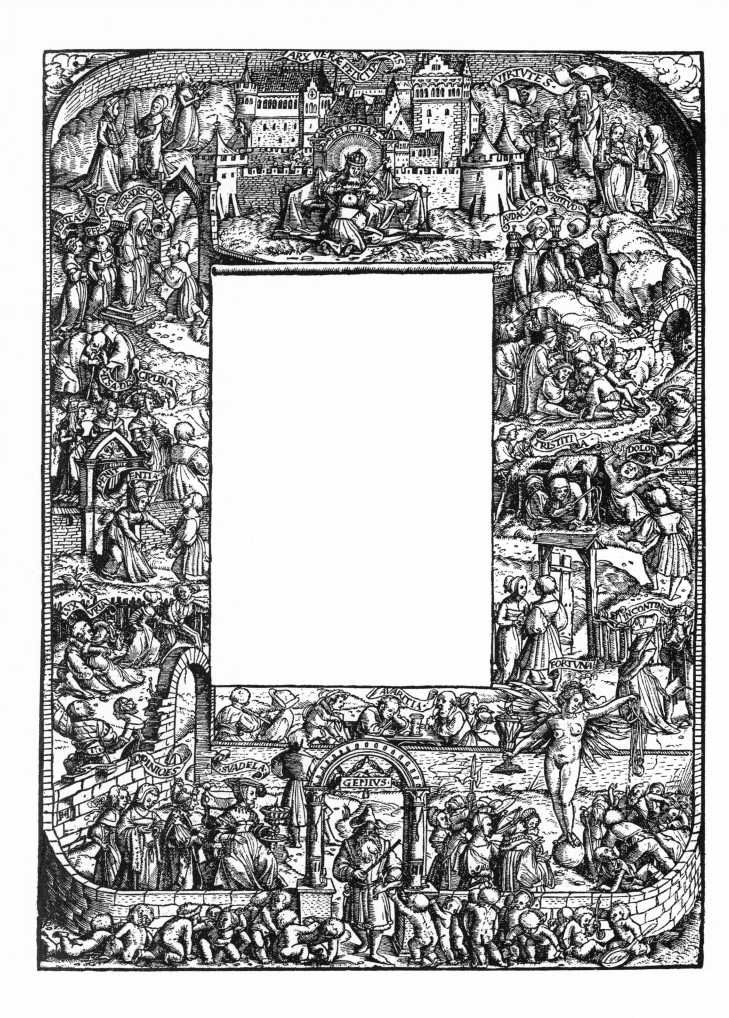

PLATE 58. *Decoration for a title page (the philosopher Cebes' theory of the path to true happiness) by Hans Holbein the Younger, from the print shop of Johann Froben, Basle. Original size.*

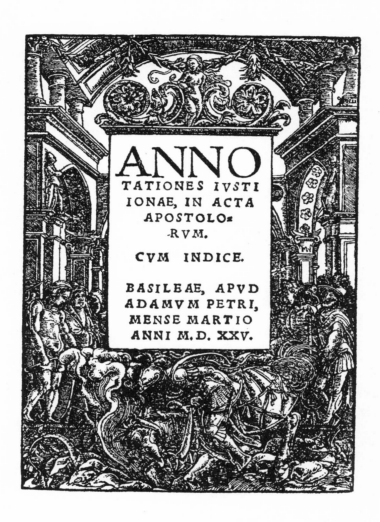

PLATE 59. *Title decoration (with Marcus Curtius riding into the gaping hole), in metal-cut, by Hans Holbein the Younger, from the print shop of Adam Petri, Basle, 1525. Original size.*

PLATE 60. *Title page (with Hercules and Orpheus) by Hans Holbein the Younger, from the print shop of Adam Petri, Basle, 1523. Original size.*

PLATE 61. *Title page (with Sts. Peter and Paul, the symbols of the Evangelists and*
Christ as master over lions) by Hans Holbein the Younger, from the print shop of
Adam Petri, Basle, ca. 1524. Original 245 × 170 mm.

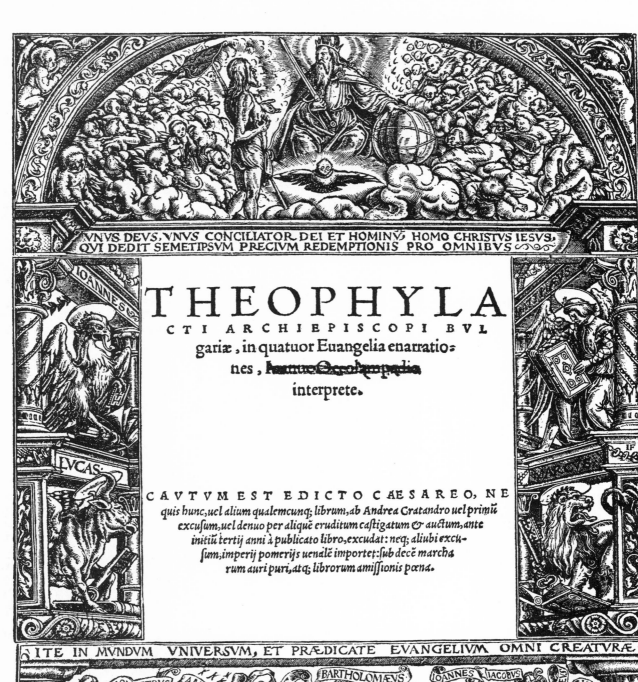

UNUS DEUS, UNUS CONCILIATOR DEI ET HOMINU HOMO CHRISTUS IESUS, QUI DEDIT SEMETIPSUM PRECIUM REDEMPTIONIS PRO OMNIBUS

THEOPHYLA
CTI ARCHIEPISCOPI BUL
gariæ, in quatuor Euangelia enarratio:
nes, ~~Ioanne Oecolampadio~~
interprete.

CAUTUM EST EDICTO CÆSAREO, NE
quis hunc, uel alium qualemcunq; librum, ab Andrea Cratandro uel primũ
excuſum, uel denuo per aliquẽ eruditum caſtigatum & auctum, ante
initiũ tertij anni à publicato libro, excudat: neq; aliubi excuſum, imperij pomerijs uenãlẽ importeʈ: ſub decẽ marcha
rum auri puri, atq; librorum amiſſionis pœna.

PLATE 62. *Title page (with the Trinity, the Evangelists and the Apostles), in metal-cut, by Master I. F., from the print shop of Andreas Cratander, Basle, 1525. Original size.*

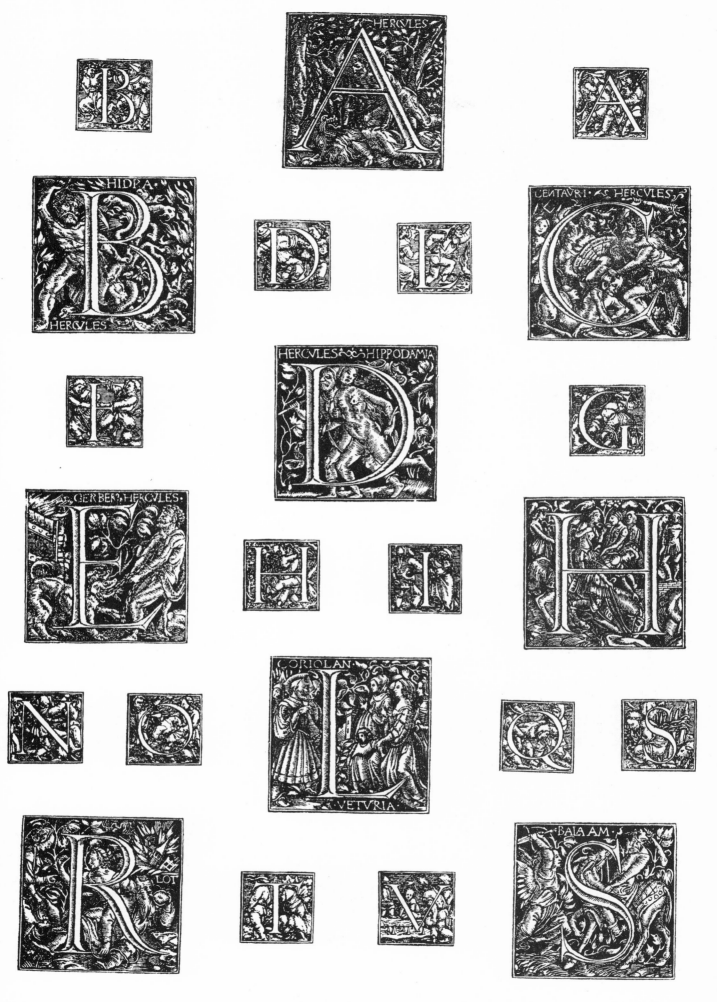

PLATE 63. *Fourteen letters from the Alphabet of Peasants by Hans Holbein the Younger and nine larger metal-cut letters by Master I. F., from the print shop of Johann Froben, Basle, 1518–1527. Original size.*

PLATE 64. *Complete small Alphabet of Children by Hans Holbein the Younger, from the print shops of Andreas Cratander and Johann Bebel, Basle, 1527–1532, and nine larger letters with children by the same artist, from the print shop of Valentin Curio, Basle, ca. 1522. All 94% of original size.*

PLATE 65. *Initials and printer's mark by Hans Holbein the Younger, from the print shop of Henric Petri, Basle, 1528, and (at bottom of plate, with horizontal hatching) initials by an artist of the Basle school, from the print shop of Johann Faber, Freiburg im Breisgau (Faber had been in Basle), ca. 1535. ¾ original size.*

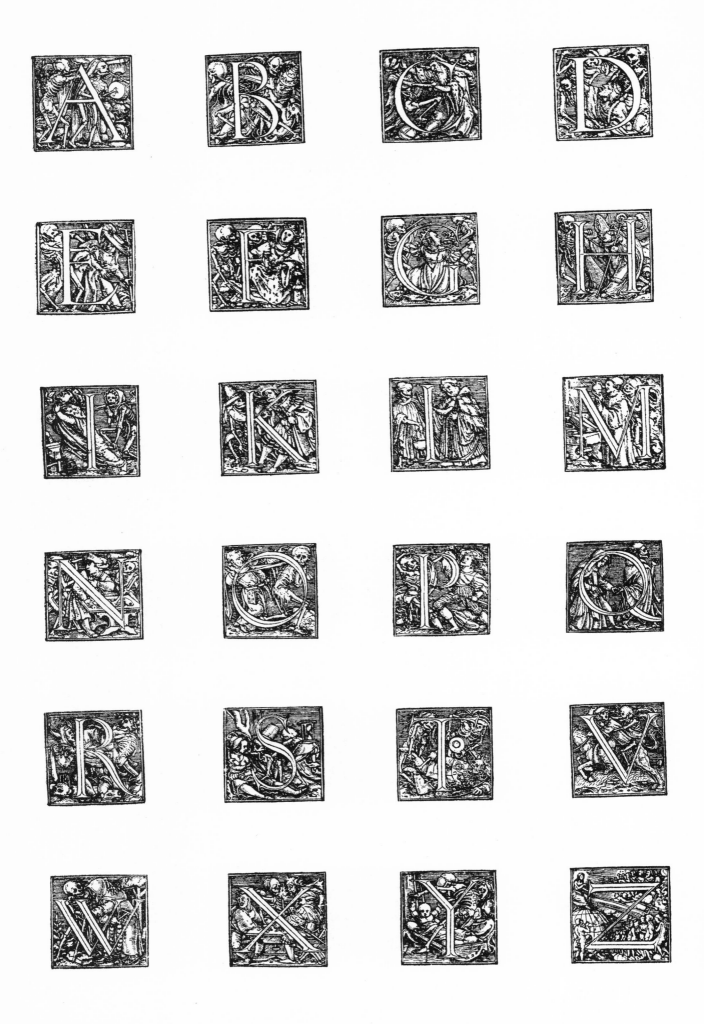

PLATE 66. *Complete Dance of Death Alphabet by Hans Holbein the Younger*, ca. *1523. Original size.*

PLATE 67. *Initials by Hans Holbein the Younger, from the print shop of Valentin Curio, Basle, ca. 1525, ⅔ original size, and printer's sign of Johann Froben, by Ambrosius Holbein, Basle, ca. 1517. Original size.*

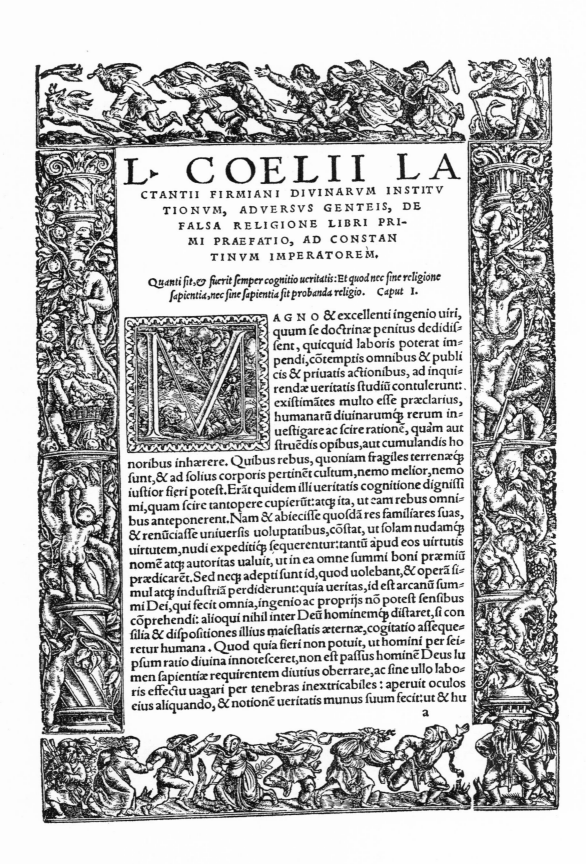

L· COELII LA
CTANTII FIRMIANI DIVINARVM INSTITV
TIONVM, ADVERSVS GENTEIS, DE
FALSA RELIGIONE LIBRI PRI
MI PRAEFATIO, AD CONSTAN
TINVM IMPERATOREM,

Quanti sit, & fuerit semper cognitio ueritatis: Et quod nec sine religione
sapientia, nec sine sapientia sit probanda religio.   Caput I.

AGNO & excellenti ingenio uiri,
quum se doctrinæ penitus dedidis=
sent, quicquid laboris poterat im=
pendi, cõtemptis omnibus & publi
cis & priuatis actionibus, ad inqui=
rendæ ueritatis studiũ contulerunt:
existimãtes multo esse præclarius,
humanarũ diuinarumᖁ rerum in=
uestigare ac scire ratione, quàm aut
struẽdis opibus, aut cumulandis ho
noribus inhærere. Quibus rebus, quoniam fragiles terrenæᖁ
sunt, & ad solius corporis pertinẽt cultum, nemo melior, nemo
iustior fieri potest. Erãt quidem illi ueritatis cognitione dignissi
mi, quam scire tantopere cupierũt: atᖁ ita, ut eam rebus omni=
bus anteponerent. Nam & abiecisse quosdã res familiares suas,
& renũciasse uniuersis uoluptatibus, cõstat, ut solam nudamᖁ
uirtutem, nudi expeditiᖁ sequerentur: tantũ àpud eos uirtutis
nomẽ atᖁ autoritas ualuit, ut in ea omne summi boni præmiũ
prædicarẽt. Sed neᖁ adepti sunt id, quod uolebant, & operã si=
mul atᖁ industriã perdiderunt: quia ueritas, id est arcanũ sum=
mi Dei, qui fecit omnia, ingenio ac proprijs nõ potest sensibus
cõprehendi: alioqui nihil inter Deũ hominemᖁ distaret, si con
silia & dispositiones illius maiestatis æternæ, cogitatio asseque=
retur humana . Quod quia fieri non potuit, ut homini per seí=
psum ratio diuina innotesceret, non est passus hominẽ Deus lu
men sapientiæ requirentem diutius oberrare, ac sine ullo labo=
ris effectu uagari per tenebras inextricabiles : aperuit oculos
eius aliquando, & notione ueritatis munus suum fecit: ut & hu

a

PLATE 68. *Decorated page, in metal-cut, by Hans Holbein the Younger (horizontal borders) and Master I. F. (vertical borders), from the print shop of Andreas Cratander and Johann Bebel, Basle, 1523. Original 243× 159 mm.*

PLATE 69. *Initials by Hans Holbein the Younger, from the print shop of Andreas Cratander and Johann Bebel, Basle, ca. 1538.* ⅔ *original size.*

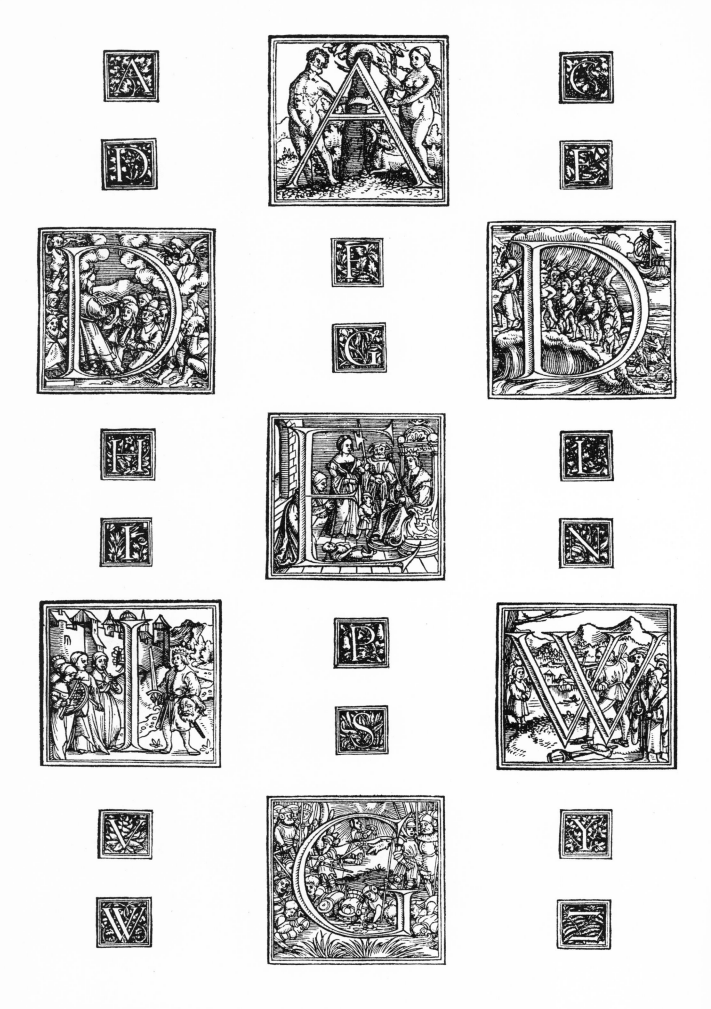

PLATE 70. *Initials from the print shop of Christoph Froschouer, Zurich, 1528. The larger ones, with scenes from Biblical and Swiss history, are perhaps by Niclas Manuel. All 96% of original size.*

PLATE 71. *Title page by Johann Wechtlin, from the print shop of Matthias Schürer, Strasbourg, 1512. Original 228 × 142 mm.*

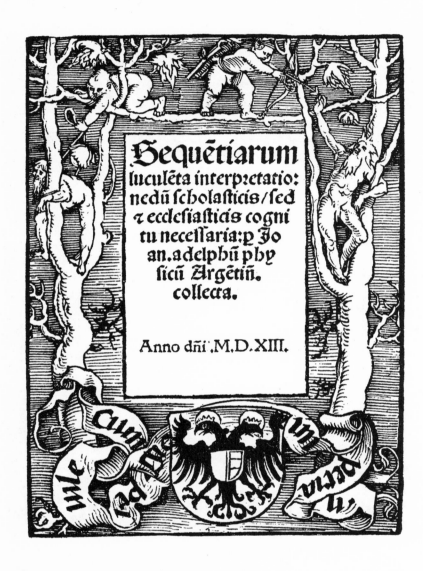

PLATE 72. *Title page by Johann Wechtlin, from the print shop of Matthias Schürer, Strasbourg, 1513. Original size.*

PLATE 73. *Title page, perhaps by Hans Baldung called Grien, from the print shop of Matthias Hupfuff, Strasbourg, 1515. Original size.*

Summa Angelica
de Casibus conscientie: cū
multis vtilibus et val-
de necessariis ad-
ditionibus no
uiter inser
tis.

M.D.XV.

PLATE 74. *Decorated page by Johann Wechtlin, from the print shop of Matthias Schürer, Strasbourg, 1515. Original 244 × 182 mm.*

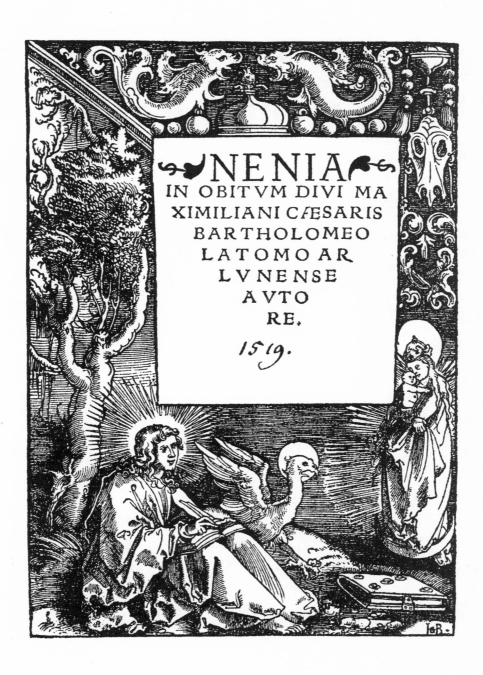

NENIA
IN OBITVM DIVI MA
XIMILIANI CÆSARIS
BARTHOLOMEO
LATOMO AR
LVNENSE
AVTO
RE.
1519.

PLATE 75. *Title page by Hans Baldung called Grien, from the print shop of Johann Knoblouch, Strasbourg, 1519. Original size.*

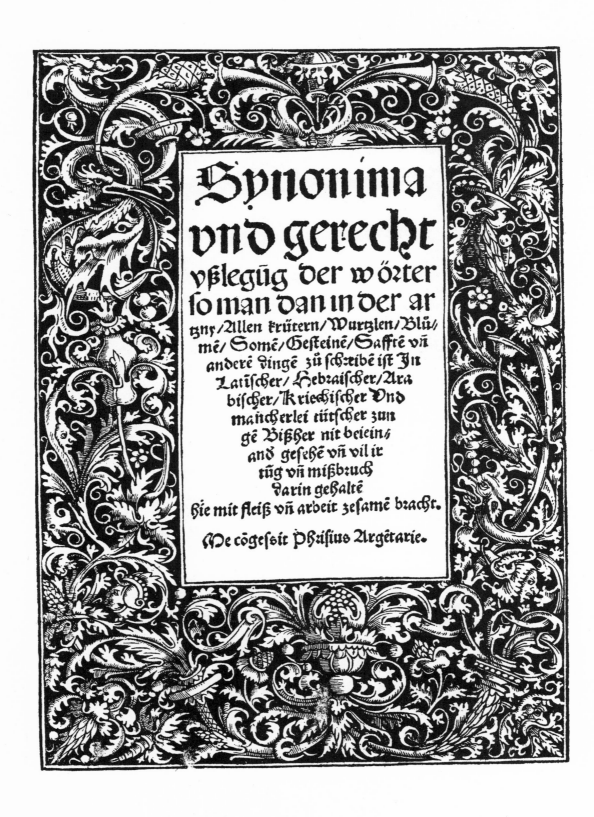

Synonima vnd gerecht vßlegüg der wörter so man dan in der arßny/Allen krütern/Wurtzlen/Blů/mê/Some/Gesteine/Saffte vñ andere dinge zů schribe ist In Latischer/Hebraischer/Arabischer/Kriechischer Vnd mancherlei tütscher zun ge Bißher nit beiein/and gesehe vñ vil ir tüg vñ mißbruch Darin gehalte hie mit fleiß vñ arbeit zesame bracht.

Me cögessit Pßisius Argetarie.

PLATE 76. *Title page by an unknown master, from the print shop of Johann Grüninger, Strasbourg, 1519. Original size.*

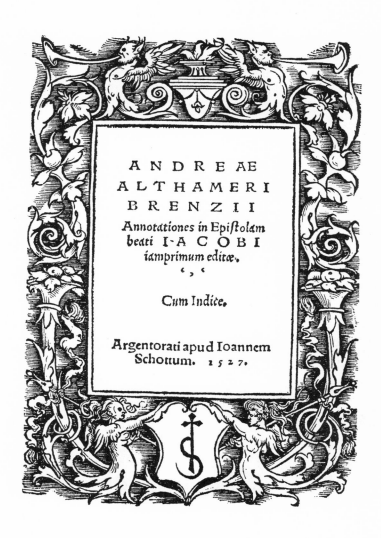

ANDREAE
ALTHAMERI
BRENZII
Annotationes in Epiſtolam
beati I·A COBI
iamprimum editæ.
' , '

Cum Indice.

Argentorati apud Ioannem
Schottum. 1527.

PLATE 77. *Title page by Hans Baldung called Grien, from the print shop of Johann Schott, Strasbourg, 1527. Original size.*

PLATE 78. *Decorative borders, perhaps by Hans Baldung called Grien, from the print shop of Wolff Köpfel, Strasbourg, 1520's. Original size.*

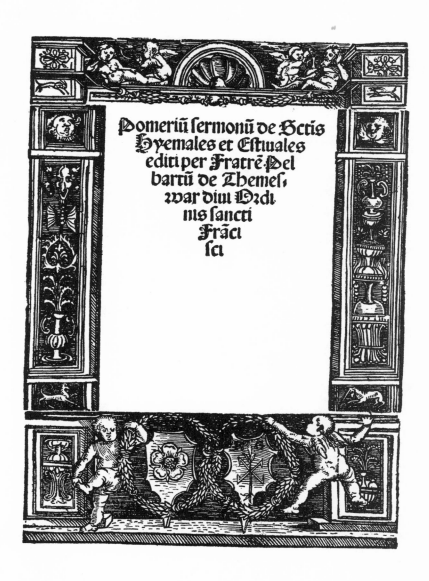

PLATE 79. *Title page by an unknown master, from the print shop of Heinrich Gran,*
Hagenau (Alsace), ca. 1510. Original 228 × 161 mm.

PLATE 80. *Initials and printer's mark (the latter by Hans Baldung called Grien),*
from the print shop of Thomas Anselm (of Baden), Hagenau, 1520.

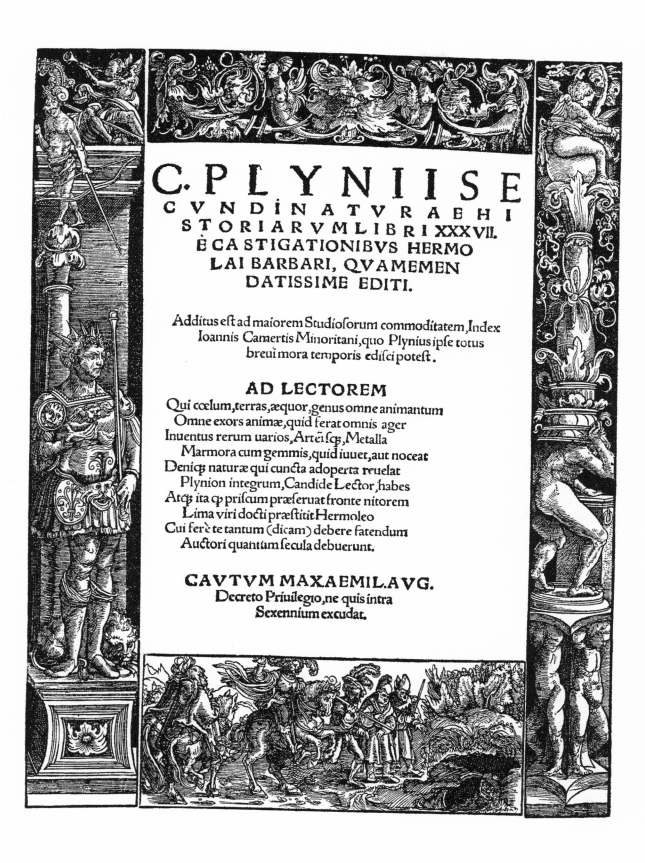

C. PLYNII SE
CVNDI NATVRAE HI
STORIARVM LIBRI XXXVII.
È CASTIGATIONIBVS HERMO
LAI BARBARI, QVAMEMEN
DATISSIME EDITI.

Additus eſt ad maiorem Studioſorum commoditatem, Index
Ioannis Camertis Minoritani, quo Plynius ipſe totus
breui mora temporis ediſci poteſt.

AD LECTOREM

Qui cœlum, terras, æquor, genus omne animantum
Omne exors animæ, quid ferat omnis ager
Inuentus rerum uarios, Artei ſcp, Metalla
Marmora cum gemmis, quid iuuet, aut noceat
Deniᷠ naturæ qui cuncta adoperta reuelat
Plynion integrum, Candide Lector, habes
Atᷠ ita cp priſcum præſeruat fronte nitorem
Lima viri docti præſtitit Hermoleo
Cui ferè te tantum (dicam) debere fatendum
Auctori quantúm ſecula debuerunt.

CAVTVM MAXAEMIL. AVG.
Decreto Priuilegio, ne quis intra
Sexennium excudat.

PLATE 81. *Title page (with Marcus Curtius) by an unknown master, from the print shop of Thomas Anselm, Hagenau, 1518. Original 269 × 195 mm.*

PLATE 82. *Initials by an unknown master, from the print shop of Johann Schöffer,*
Mainz, 1518. Original size.

PLATE 83. *Initials by an unknown master, from the print shop of Johann Schöffer, Mainz, 1518. Original size.*

PLATE 84. *Initials by an unknown master, from the print shop of Johann Schöffer, Mainz, 1518. Original size.*

PLATE 85. *Initials and Schöffer's mark by an unknown master, from the print shop of Johann Schöffer, Mainz, 1518. Original size.*

AD REVEREN

DISS. IN CHRISTO PATREM ILLVSTRISS
PRINCIPEM ALBERTVM BRANDEN
burgen̄. Cardinalem Archiepiscopum Moguntin̄. & Magde‐
burgen̄. Principem electorem, primatemꝗ, VLRICHI
Hutteni Equ. in Titum Liuium historicum, libris
auctum duobus, Præfatio.

VCTVS NVPER, RECVPERA‐
ta quadam minime contemnenda sui parte T. Liuius, cum secum ipse consultaret, ubi, & cuius sub inscriptione in lucem exiret, hanc nostram si‐ bi delegit auream Moguntiam, pater ac princeps colendissime, inter alias Europæ urbes dignissi‐ mā ratus arbitror, ubi renasci gauderet, tuáque perspecta ingēti erga studiosos ac literatos omes benignitate, aptū se inuenisse putauit principē, cuius auspicijs prodire in publicum, ac mūdo se ostēdere uellet. Illę scilicet aut cogitauit hæc, aut non inepte à nobis cogitasse putari debet. Nam si uel locū uoluit Liuius ali‐ quem suo decorare egressu, quem debuit urbi, artis omnium quæ usquam sunt, aut unquam fuerunt præstantissimæ inuētrici, ac alumnæ (impressorā puto, quam hæc dedit) præferre? Vel hominem deligere sibi, cuius impres‐ sum fronti suæ nomen, ueluti temporis monetam, quoquo ire contingat, ho‐ noris caussa præferret, alium certe maluisse neminē crediderimus quàm te, cuius in euehendis literarum studijs, ac augendo optimarum disciplinarum cultu, incredibilis ardor ac mira industria, in percolendis uero doctis homi‐ nibus immēsa liberalitas ac regia plane munificētia. Hæc efficiunt, ut omnes quotquot sumus aut hominum opinione docti, aut re uera recte studiosi, ad unum hoc quoddam uelut asylum confugiamus, quanquam tu nō susti‐ nes confugientes nos, uerū cunctantes ad te ultro rapis. Possem hic referre, quos uiros, quàm tu familiariter accersiueris, quæ dona alijs dederis, quanta multis pollicitus sis, quomodo pecunia pariter ac dignitate nonnullos au‐ xeris, & tua aula ut aperta sit doctis hospitalissime uiris, nisi scirem multum à tua alienum esse modestia, in Liuij præfatione tuarū tibi laudum encomiū legi. Certe profecto & locus est opportunus hic, ubi non renasci tantum uelit eximius scriptor, sed oriri etiam olim potuerit, & tu dignus, qui patronum in uulgo Liuij agas. Neꝗ uicissim (ut tua fretus bonitate dicā aliquid libere) indignus ille qui tibi offeratur, tibiꝗ dedicetur, ac tuo qui prætento nomine in manibus habeatur. Quinetiā si liberius adhuc audire me sustines, dicam

a ij   non

PLATE 86. *Decorated border, in metal-cut, by an unknown master, from the print shop of Johann Schöffer, Mainz, 1518. Original size.*

Herr Erasmus von Roterdam verteutschte außlegůg über disen spruch Christi vnsers Herrñ Matthei am dreyundzweintzigsten Capittel/ vonn den Phariseyerñ/ Sie thun alle ire werck/ das sie von den menschen gesehen werden/ Vnd breyten jr gebottzedeln auß.

¶ Vom heyltumb ꝛc.

1521.

PLATE 87. *Title page by an unknown master, from the print shop of Johann Schöffer Mainz, 1521. Original size.*

PLATE 88. *Letters from alphabet after designs by Albrecht Dürer, from the print shop of Eucharius Hirtzhorn, Cologne, 1524. Original size.*

PLATE 89. *Letters from alphabet after designs by Albrecht Dürer, from the print shop of Eucharius Hirtzhorn, Cologne, 1524. Original size.*

PLATE 90. *Letters from alphabet after designs by Albrecht Dürer, from the print shop of Eucharius Hirtzhorn, Cologne, 1524. Original size.*

ℒ HERODOTI

HALICARNÆSSEI HISTO
RIOGRAPHI LIBRI NO
VEM, MVSARVM NO
MINIBVS IN-
SCRIPTI,
INTERPRETE LAVREN. VAL.

ACCESSERVNT huic editioni plus minus nouem fo-
lia, quæ in primo lib. à Laurentio exemplaris forte uitio præ-
termiſſa, iam primum à Conrado Heresbachio è græco ſuis lo
cis ſunt adiecta, cum alia haudquaquã pœnitenda in cæteris li
bris acceſſione caſtigationeǫ; ad Græcum exemplar facta, id
quod diligens lector conferendo facile deprehendet.

ITEM De genere uitáǫ; Homeri libellus, iam primum ab eo
dem Heresbachio è græco in latinum conuerſus.

In Herod MVSAS epigramma.

ἰῶτος, μ᾿ῦσας ὑπέδ᾿εξατο, τῷ δ᾿ἀϛ ἑκάϛη
ἀντὶ Φιλοξενίης βίϛλον ἔδωκε μίην.

Anno M. D. XXVI.

Sub edicto & priuilegio Cæf. ad quadriennium.

PLATE 92. *Alphabet of Children by Anton von Worms, from the print shop of Peter Quentell, Cologne, 1530. Original size.*

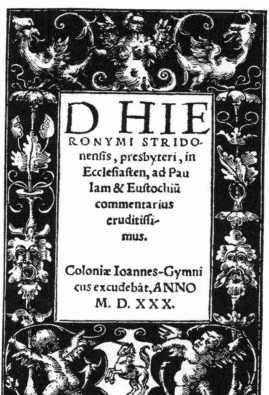

PLATE 93. *Title page by a master of the Cologne school, from the print shop of Johann Gymnicus, Cologne, 1530, and initials (all but the larger M, from the print shop of Johann Schöffer, Mainz) by Anton von Worms, from the print shop of Peter Quentell and Melchior Novesanius, Cologne 1530–1536. All ¾ original size.*

PLATE 94. *Letters from the large Alphabet of Children by Anton von Worms, from the print shop of Melchior Novesanius, Cologne, ca. 1535; a large S and H by the same artist, from the print shop of Peter Quentell, Cologne, 1530–1536; an M from the print shop of Johann Schöffer, Mainz, ca. 1518. All ¾ original size.*

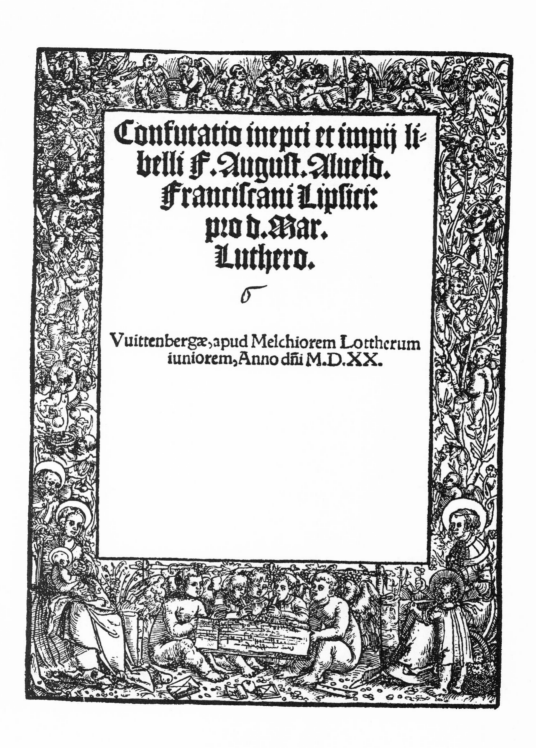

Confutatio inepti et impij libelli F. Auguſt. Alueld. Franciſcani Lipſici: p͛o d. Mar. Luthero.

Vuittenbergæ, apud Melchiorem Lottherum iuniorem, Anno dñi M.D.XX.

PLATE 95. *Title page by Lucas Cranach the Elder, from the print shop of Melchior Lotter, Wittenberg, 1520. Original size.*

Biblia noua
Aluelde=
fis.

Wittenbergae.
ANNO M. D. XX.

PLATE 96. *Title page by Lucas Cranach the Elder, from the print shop of Johann Grünenberg, Wittenberg, 1520. Original size.*

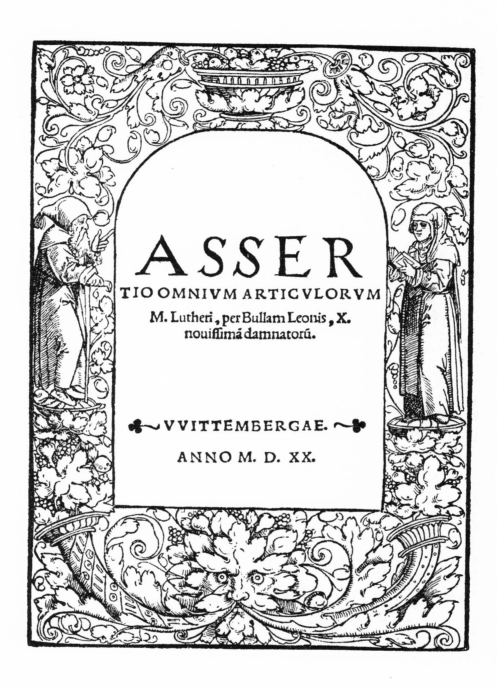

ASSER
TIO OMNIVM ARTICVLORVM
M. Lutheri, per Bullam Leonis, X.
nouissimã damnatorũ.

❧⟶ VVITTEMBERGAE. ⟶❧

ANNO M. D. XX.

PLATE 97. *Title page by Lucas Cranach the Elder, from the print shop of Johann Grünenberg, Wittenberg, 1520. Original size.*

HIERO
NYMI ECLOGA DE
LOCIS HEBRAICIS.

VVITTEMBERGAE.

PLATE 98. *Title page by Lucas Cranach the Elder, from the print shop of Johann Grünenberg, Wittenberg, 1522. Original size.*

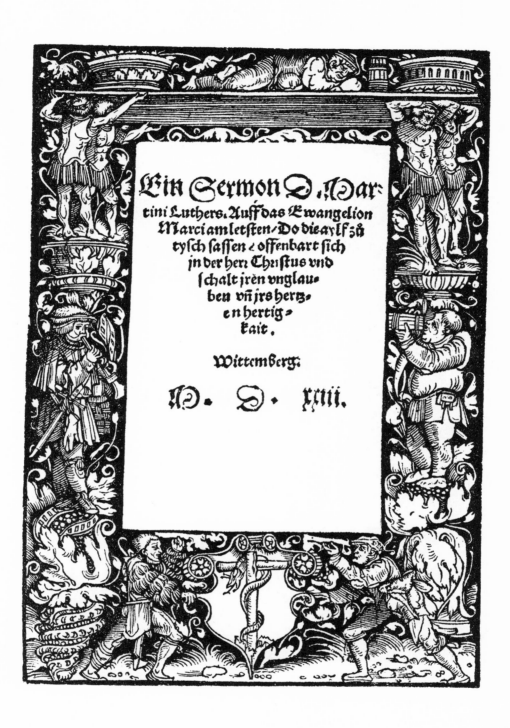

PLATE 99. *Title page from a sermon by Luther, designed by Lucas Cranach the Elder, from the print shop of Georg Rhaw, Wittenberg, 1523. Original size.*

PLATE 100. *Title page from another work by Martin Luther, designed by Lucas Cranach the Elder, from the print shop of Melchior Lotter, Wittenberg, 1527. Original size.*

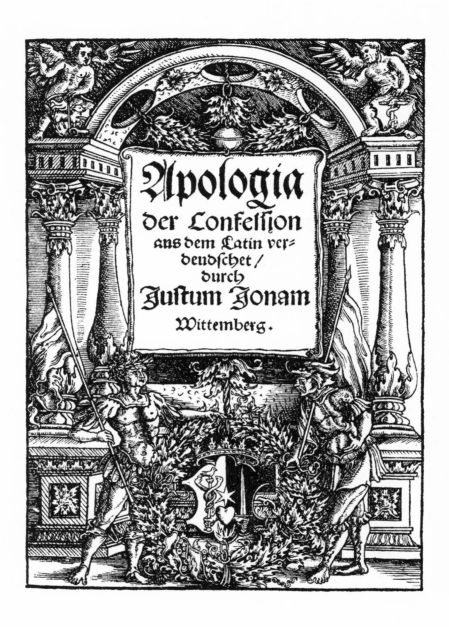

PLATE 101. *Title page by Lucas Cranach the Elder, from the print shop of Georg Rhaw, Wittenberg, 1531. Original size.*

PLATE 102. *Initials by Lucas Cranach the Elder, from the print shop of Hans Lufft, Wittenberg, 1534, and (only the large D) from an unknown print shop in Leipzig, ca. 1512.*

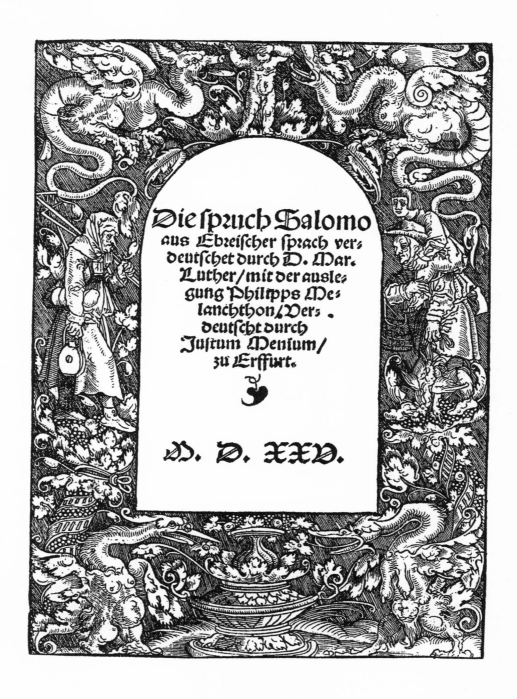

Die spruch Salomo
aus Ebreischer sprach ver=
deutschet durch D. Mar.
Luther/mit der ausle=
gung Philipps Me=
lanchthon/Ver=
deutscht durch
Justum Menium/
zu Erffurt.

M. D. XXV.

PLATE 103. *Title page by an unknown master, from the print shop of Michael Sachs ("at the Sign of the Leopard"), Erfurt, 1525. Original size. The book is Luther's translation of Proverbs with Melanchthon's commentary.*

PLATE 104. *Initials, in metal-cut, by Geofroy Tory, from the print shop of Robert Estienne, Paris, ca. 1536. ¾ original size.*

PLATE 105. *Initials, in metal-cut, by Geofroy Tory, from the print shop of Robert Estienne, Paris, ca. 1536. ¾ original size.*

PLATE 106. *Greek initials, in metal-cut, by Geofroy Tory, from the print shop of Robert Estienne, Paris, ca. 1536.* ¾ *original size.*

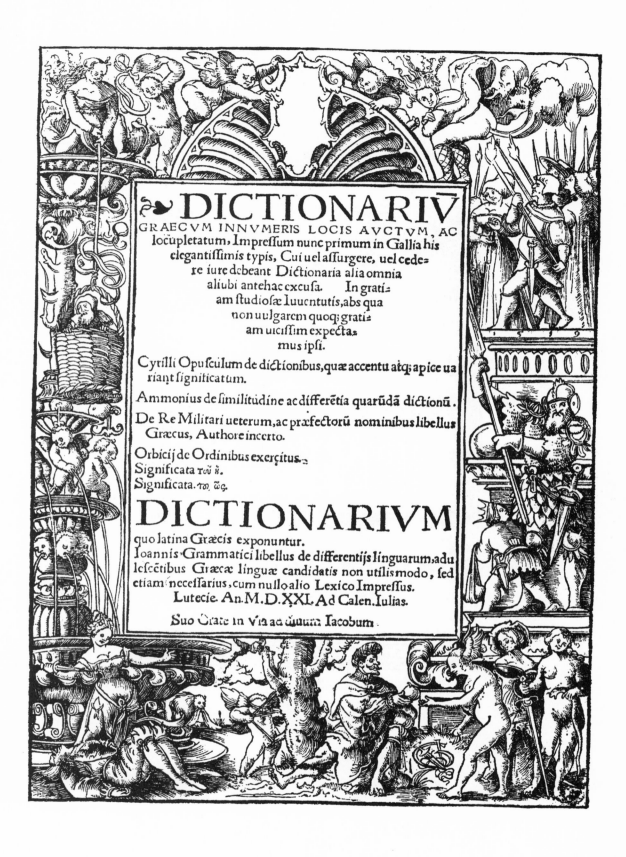

DICTIONARIV

GRAECVM INNVMERIS LOCIS AVCTVM, AC
locupletatum, Impreſſum nunc primum in Gallia his
elegantiſſimis typis, Cui uel aſſurgere, uel cede=
re iure debeant Dictionaria alia omnia
aliubi antehac excuſa.   In grati=
am ſtudioſæ Iuuentutis, abs qua
non uulgarem quoq; grati=
am uiciſſim expecta=
mus ipſi.

Cyrilli Opuſculum de dictionibus, quæ accentu atq; apice ua
riant ſignificatum.

Ammonius de ſimilitudine ac differētia quarūdā dictionū.

De Re Militari ueterum, ac præfectorū nominibus libellus
Græcus, Authore incerto.

Orbicij de Ordinibus exercitus.
Significata τοῦ ῆ.
Significata. τω. ῶς.

DICTIONARIVM

quo latina Græcis exponuntur.
Ioannis·Grammatici libellus de differentijs linguarum, adu
leſcētibus Græcæ linguæ candidatis non utilis modo, ſed
etiam neceſſarius, cum nullo alio Lexico Impreſſus.
Lutecie. An. M. D. XXI. Ad Calen. Iulias.

Suo Grate in via ad diuum Iacobum.

PLATE 107. *Title page (with Pyramus and Thisbe, the Judgment of Paris, David and Goliath, and Virgil as magician) by Urs Graf, from the print shop of Johann Badius, Paris, 1521. Original size.*

PLATE 108. *Bookseller's or printer's mark, from the print shop of the brothers Bernardino and Matteo Veneti, Venice, 1498. Original size.*

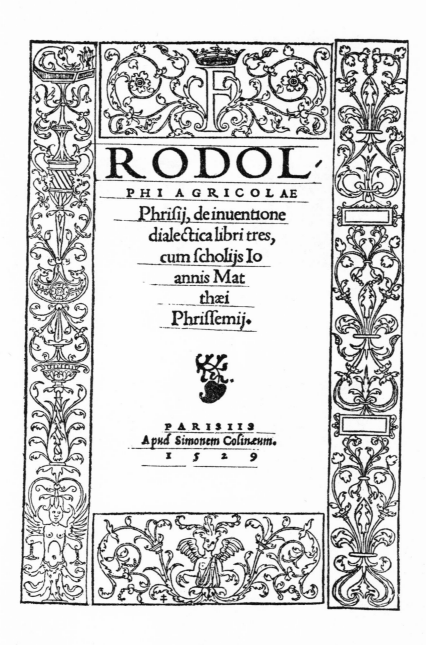

F

RODOL‑
PHI AGRICOLAE
Phrifij, de inuentione
dialectica libri tres,
cum fcholijs Io
annis Mat
thæi
Phriffemij.

PARISIIS
Apud Simonem Colinæum.
1 5 2 9

PLATE 109. *Title page by Geofroy Tory, from the print shop of Simon de Colines.*
Paris, 1529. Original size.

PLATE 110. *Initials, in metal-cut, by Geofroy Tory, from the print shop of Simon de Colines, Paris, 1521. Original size.*

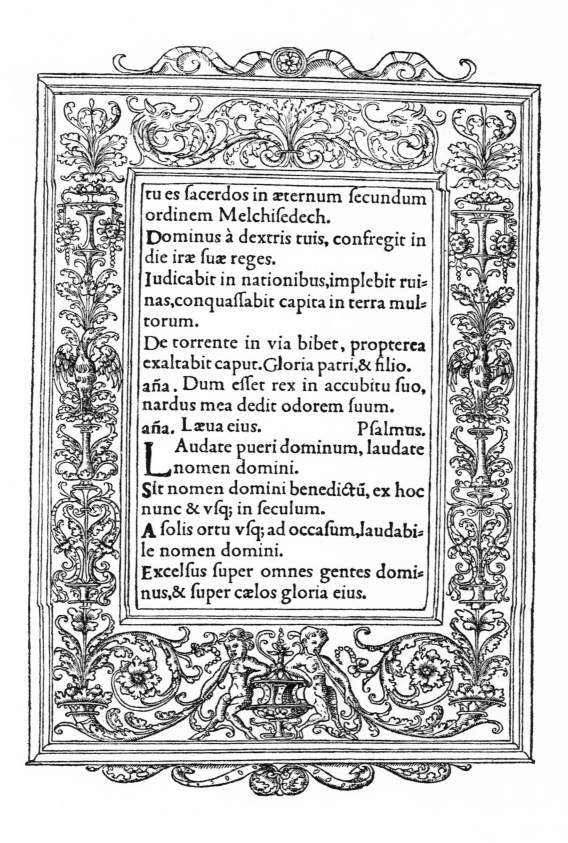

tu es sacerdos in æternum secundum ordinem Melchisedech.

Dominus à dextris tuis, confregit in die iræ suæ reges.

Iudicabit in nationibus, implebit ruinas, conquassabit capita in terra multorum.

De torrente in via bibet, propterea exaltabit caput. Gloria patri, & filio.

aña. Dum esset rex in accubitu suo, nardus mea dedit odorem suum.

aña. Læua eius.   Psalmus.

LAudate pueri dominum, laudate nomen domini.

Sit nomen domini benedictũ, ex hoc nunc & vsq; in seculum.

A solis ortu vsq; ad occasum, laudabile nomen domini.

Excelsus super omnes gentes dominus, & super cælos gloria eius.

PLATE III. *Decorated pages, from a Book of Hours, by Geofroy Tory, from the print shop of Simon de Colines, Paris, ca. 1540. Original size.*

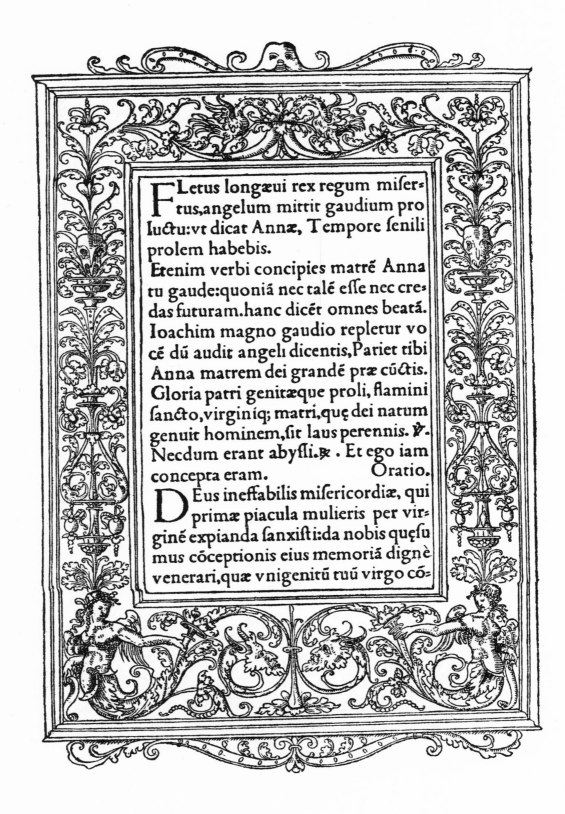

PLATE 112. *Decorated page, from a Book of Hours, by Geofroy Tory, from the print shop of Simon de Colines, Paris, ca. 1540. Original size.*

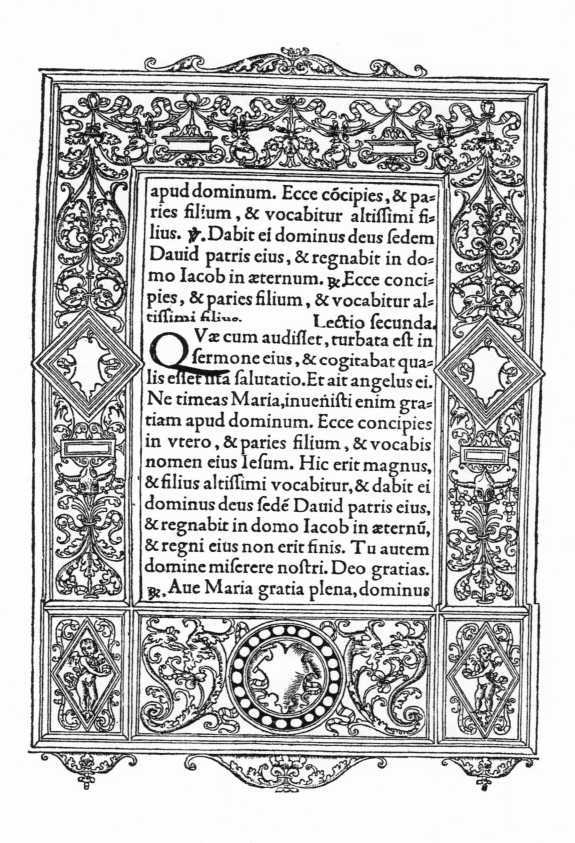

apud dominum. Ecce cócipies, & pa=
ries filium , & vocabitur altiſſimi fi=
lius. ℣.Dabit ei dominus deus ſedem
Dauid patris eius, & regnabit in do=
mo Iacob in æternum. ℞.Ecce conci=
pies, & paries filium , & vocabitur al=
tiſſimi filius.　　　　Lectio ſecunda.
Qvæ cum audiſſet, turbata eſt in
ſermone eius , & cogitabat qua=
lis eſſet iſta ſalutatio.Et ait angelus ei.
Ne timeas Maria,inueñiſti enim gra=
tiam apud dominum. Ecce concipies
in vtero, & paries filium , & vocabis
nomen eius Ieſum. Hic erit magnus,
& filius altiſſimi vocabitur,& dabit ei
dominus deus ſedé Dauid patris eius,
& regnabit in domo Iacob in æternū,
& regni eius non erit finis. Tu autem
domine miſerere noſtri. Deo gratias.
℞, Aue Maria gratia plena, dominus

PLATE 113. *Decorated page, from a Book of Hours, by Geofroy Tory, from the print
shop of Simon de Colines, Paris, ca. 1540. Original size.*

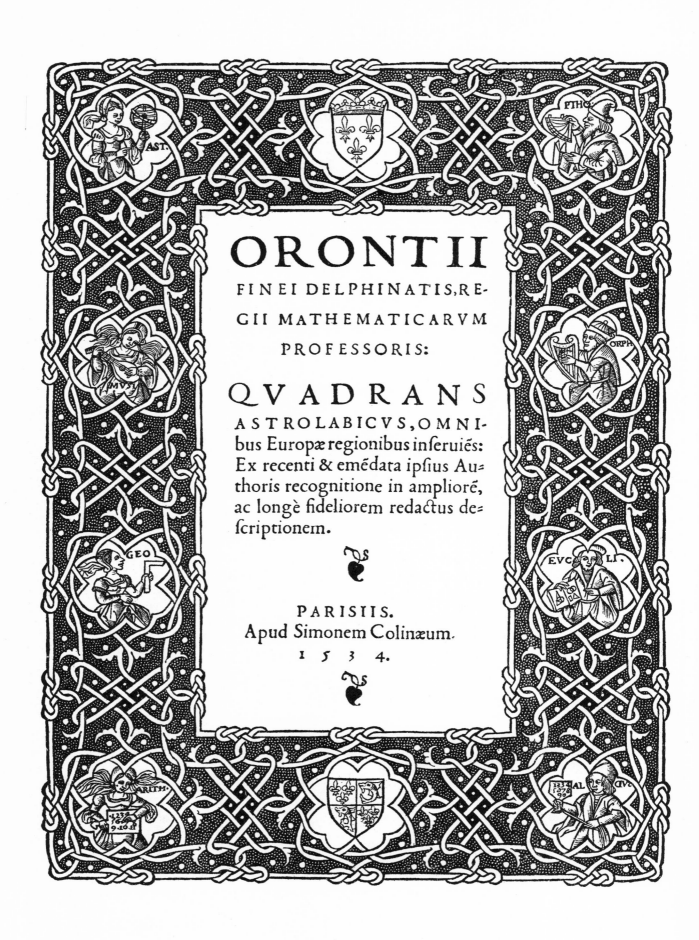

ORONTII

FINEI DELPHINATIS, RE-
GII MATHEMATICARVM
PROFESSORIS:

QVADRANS

ASTROLABICVS, OMNI-
bus Europæ regionibus inferuiés:
Ex recenti & emédata ipfius Au-
thoris recognitione in amplioré,
ac longè fideliorem redactus de=
fcriptionem.

PARISIIS.
Apud Simonem Colinæum.
1 5 3 4.

PLATE 114. *Decorated title page by Oronce Fine, from the print shop of Simon de Colines, Paris, 1534.*

Orontij Finei Del

PHINATIS, REGII
Mathematicarum
professoris,

IN SEX PRIORES LIBROS
geometricorum elementorum
Euclidis Megarensis De=
monstrationes.

Quibus ipsius Euclidis textus græcus, suis lo·
cis insertus est:vna cum interpretatione
latina Bartholamæi Zamberti Ve·
neti,ad fidem geometricã per
eundem Orontium
recognita.

CVM PRIVILEGIO
Regis ad decennium,

PARISIIS.
Apud Simonem Colinæum.
1 5 3 6.

Virescit vulnere virtus.

PLATE 115. *Decorated title page by Oronce Fine, from the print shop of Simon de Colines, Paris, 1536. Original size.*

PLATE 116. *Decorated title page from a work by the Humanist Guillaume Budé,*
designed by Oronce Fine, from the print shop of Michel Vascosan, Paris, 1536.
Original size.

PLATE 117. *Initials by Oronce Fine, from the print shop of Michel Vascosan, Paris, 1532. Original size.*

PLATE 118. *Initials by Oronce Fine (with a self-portrait in the O), from the print shop of Michel Vascosan, Paris, 1532. Original size.*

PLATE 119. *Various decorative borders from French and Italian print shops. Reading downward, the first and seventh are by an artist of the school of Geofroy Tory, from the print shop of Robert Estienne, Paris; the second is by Oronce Fine, 1532; the third is from the shop of Lucantonio Giunta, Venice, late 1530's; the fourth is from the shop of Michel Sonnius, Paris, 1570's and 1580's; the fifth is by an artist of the school of Bernard Salomon, from the shop of Jean de Tournes, Lyons, 1560's; the sixth is by an artist of the same school, from the shop of Antoine Vincenti, Lyons, 1560's. All 91% of original size.*

PLATE 120. *Initials, an ornament and Charles Estienne's printer's mark by an unknown master of the school of Tory, from the print shop of Charles Estienne, Paris, 1545. Original size.*

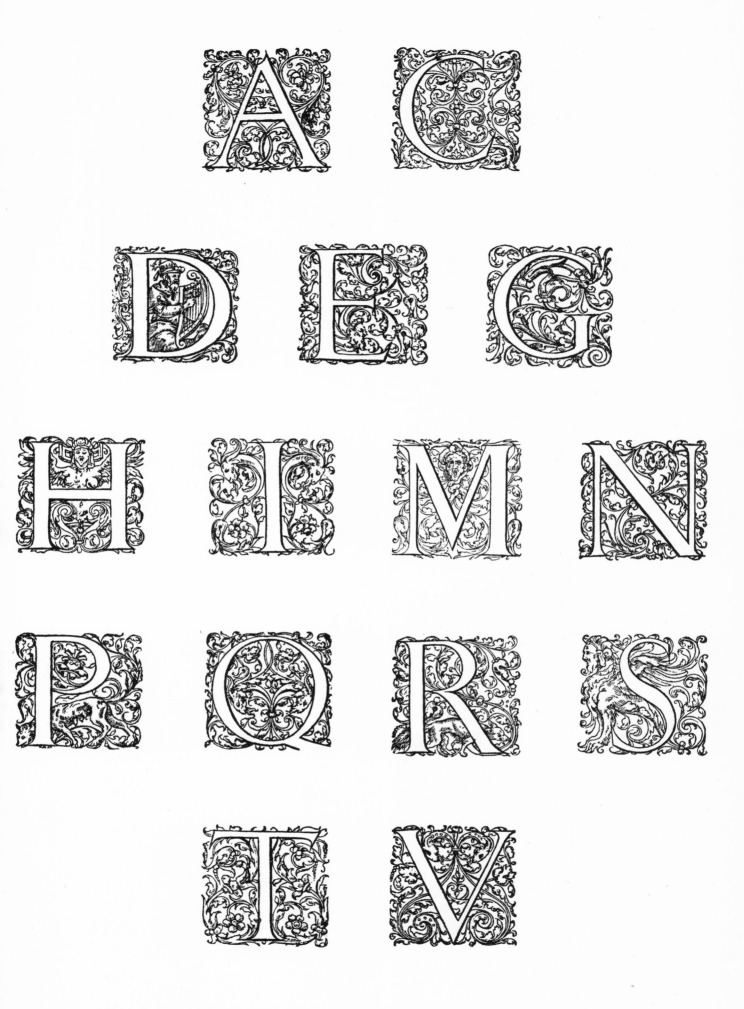

PLATE 121. *Initials by an unknown master of the school of Geofroy Tory, from the print shop of Charles Estienne, Paris, 1545. Original size.*

PLATE 122. *Initials and decorative borders by an unknown master of the school of Geofroy Tory, from the print shop of Charles Estienne, Paris, 1545. Original size.*

PLATE 123. *Initials by an unknown master, from the print shop of Philippe Rithove, Paris, 1552. Original size.*

PLATE 124. *Complete alphabet by an unknown master, from the print shop of Sébastien Nivelle, Paris, 1572; also, bookseller's mark of Jean Ruelle, Paris, 1574. All original size.*

Noli altum sapere.

Prelum
Ascēsianū

Vænundantur in ædibus Ascensianis.

PLATE 125. ABOVE: *Printer's mark by Geofroy Tory, for Robert Estienne, Paris, 1527.* BELOW: *Mark, perhaps by Albrecht Dürer, of the typographer Josse Bade (d'Asc), Paris, 1520. Both original size.*

PLATE 126. ABOVE: *Printer's mark of Jean Roigny (son-in-law of Josse Bade) by an unknown master, Paris, 1550.* BELOW: *Mark of the typographer Guillaume Desboys, Paris, 1565. Both original size.*

PLATE 127. ABOVE, LEFT TO RIGHT: *Mark of Guillaume Morel, printer of Greek to the court in Paris, 1543–1564; mark of the printers Antoine Vincenti and Hugues de la Porte, Lyons, when they joined forces in the early 1550's; mark of the printer Vincenti in the 1560's.* BELOW: *Mark of the printer de la Porte, 1559. All 95% of original size.*

PLATE 128. *Initials by an unknown Parisian typographer, used in the 1584 French edition of the works of Plutarch, published by Abel Angelier. Original size.*

PLATE 129. *Initials by an unknown Parisian typographer, used in the 1584 French edition of the works of Plutarch published by Abel Angelier. Also, some ornaments from the print shop of Frédéric Morel, Paris, 1578. All original size.*

PLATE 130. ABOVE: *Mark (with examples of filial piety, including Tobias and Aeneas) of Sébastien Nivelle, Paris, 1572.* BELOW: *Mark of Clément Baudin, Lyons, 1570. Both 98% of original size.*

CHRONIQVE DE SAVOYE,

Extraicte pour la pluspart de l'histoire de M. Guillaume Paradin.

Troisieme edition, enrichie & augmentee en divers endroits, & continuee iusques à la paix de l'an 1601.

QVOD TIBI FIERI NON VIS, ALTERI NE FECERIS.

DE L'IMPRIMERIE DE IEAN DE TOVRNES. M. DCII.

Auec priuilege du Roy.

PLATE 131. *Decorated border from the print shop of Jean de Tournes (of Lyons, later in Geneva), 1602 (the design was used as early as 1549). Original size.*

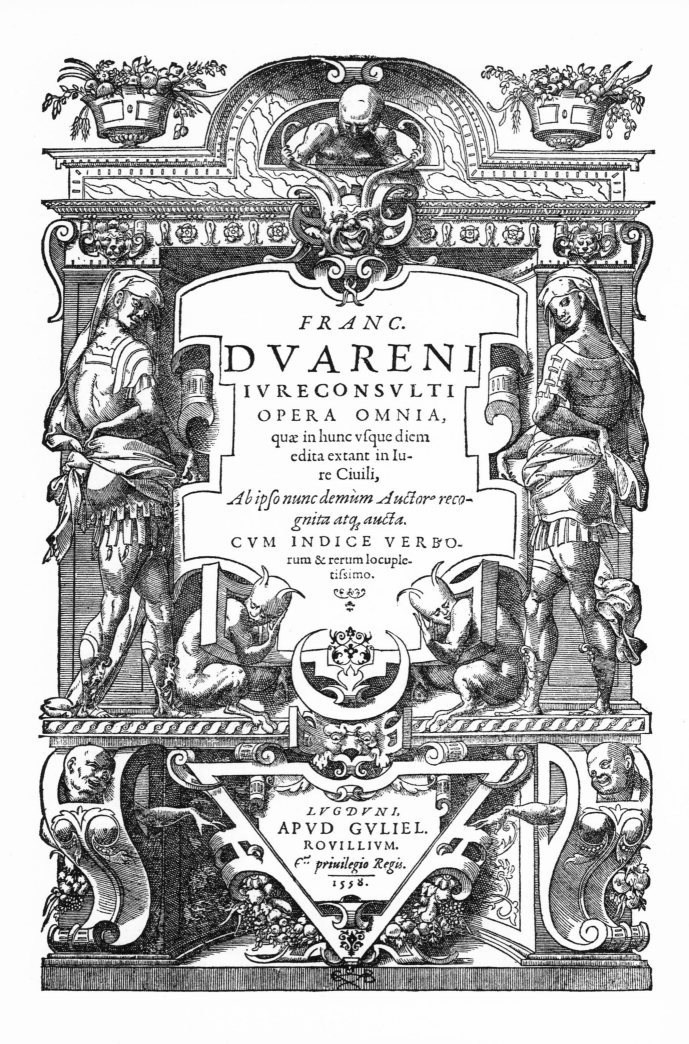

FRANC.
DVARENI
IVRECONSVLTI
OPERA OMNIA,
quæ in hunc vſque diem
edita extant in Iu-
re Ciuili,
Ab ipſo nunc demùm Auctore reco-
gnita atq̃ aucta.
CVM INDICE VERBO-
rum & rerum locuple-
tiſsimo.

LVGDVNI,
APVD GVLIEL.
ROVILLIVM.
Cū priuilegio Regis.
1558.

PLATE 132. *Title page by the artist with the monogram C B (Claude Bézoard?), from*
the print shop of Guillaume Roville, Lyons, 1558. Original size.

Arethuse en Alpheus.

Arethufa moe van taghen ghinck huer bayen
In coele reuieren met bladers ouerdect:
Alpheus volgse. ten baet noch loopen noch crayen,
Tot dat Zy van moetheyt huer aermen vuytghereckt
Heeft: Zy was van Dianens de Goddinnens sect:
Sy bidt dat Zy huer Zou willen bringhen succonrs:
Diane verhoort huer bee. Zen es niet ontscheeckt.
Maer met de wolcke was benomen Zynen cours.

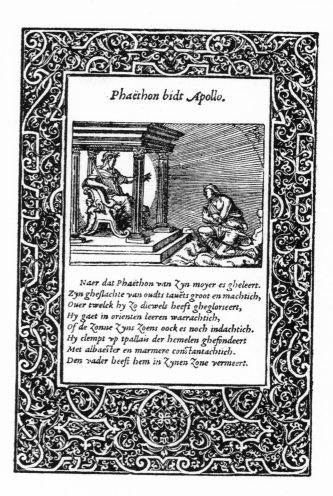

Phaëthon bidt Apollo.

Naer dat Phaëthon van Zyn moyer es gheleert.
Zyn gheslachte van oudts tauëts groot en machtich,
Ouer twelck hy Zo dicwels heeft gheglorieert,
Hy gaet in orienten leeren waerachtich,
Of de Zonne Zyns Zoens oock es noch indachtich.
Hy clempt vp tpallais der hemelen ghefondeert
Met albaester en marmere constantachtich.
Den vader heeft hem in Zynen Zone vermeert.

Pallas en Muse.

Pallas vertelt de cause van huer viage.
Huer neghen camerieren: met luyten, herpen,
Snaren gheclanck Zinghend en makende rage.
Onder al dander Zegtse datter met scheerpen
Hoeffsers een claere fonteyne gheweerpen
Es miraculeux, coel, en daer toe delicaet
Van Pegasus een peert ghe vlueghelt met strepen,
Sy gaet possessie nemen uaer hueren staet.

e

Venus, Cupido, Pluto.

Pluton en was trycke van Venus niet subiect
Noch Ceres de goddinne vanden coorene,
Dus gheeftse raedt hueren Zone die es protect
Onder huer dat hy de pyl met sceerp boorene
Zou willen schieten in thert Zonder toorene
Van Pluto. Want onder huerlieder ditie
Staet eerd, hemel, dus resteerter te stierene
Pluto tot Zuuer liefde Zonder vitie.

e 1

PLATE 133. *Decorations by Bernard Salomon for a Low German edition of Ovid's* Metamorphoses, *from the print shop of Jean de Tournes, Lyons, 1557. 96% of original size.*

Pandion, Tereus, Philomela.

Pandion Zurchuuldich van Zyn dochters heere,
Beueelt Tereus de wysheyt ende de Zurghe.
Tereus vedanck hemvan Zyn goe ionste Zeere:
Ende blyft voor Zyn twee dochters heere burghe.
Maer hy vileyn Zal vallen int schip te rugghe,
Als hy de proye vast heeft tsynder beliefte.
O Philomela waerdy toch noch niet vlugghe,
Ghy Zout vry Zyn van Zyn begheerlicke griefte.

Iuno ende de drye furien.

Ter causen van Iö benydet tgheslachte
Van Cadmus Iuno : Z y Zoust al om vitie
(Meend ick dat in gode was Zo quaet ghedachte?)
Huer selfs en es niet souffisant impulsie,
Emhuer wreede potentie ende lesie
Nemaer Zouct hulp' om Athamas prosperiteyt
Neer te legghen(hy was van de genesie
Van Cadmus)dry furien Zyn haer haest bereyt.

Thisbe verschrict huer inde leuwinne

Thisbe gheinslammeert van Cupidoens pylen
Heeft leeren spreken met wincken ende teecken,
Dus heeft huer lief huer ghesteli Zekere wylen
Ea stonden an een fonteyn om hem te spreecken.
Zy Zach een leeuwinne staen tusschen de beecken:
(Twas nacht)Zy bedect huer in drousue speluncke.
Zy liet vallen huer cleet,en en dorst niet reecken:
De leeuwinne crauwet tcleet,en gaet al proncken.

d 2

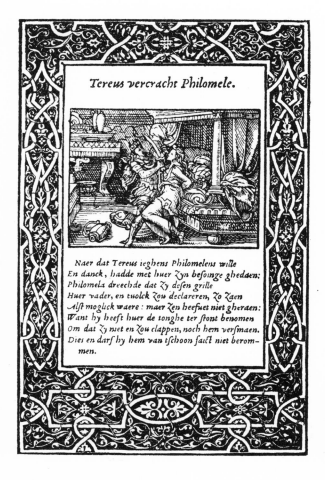

Tereus vercracht Philomele.

Naer dat Tereus ieghens Philomelens wille
En danck, hadde met huer Zyn besoinge ghedaen;
Philomela dreechde dat Zy desen grille
Huer vader, en twolck Zou declareren, Zo Zaen
Alst moghck waere : maer Zen heefuet niet gheraen:
Want hy heeft huer de tonghe ter stont benomen
Om dat Zy niet en Zou clappen, noch hem versmaen.
Dies en darf hy hem van tschoon sact niet berom-
men.

PLATE 134. *Decorations by Bernard Salomon for a Low German edition of Ovid's* Metamorphoses, *from the print shop of Jean de Tournes, Lyons, 1557. 96% of original size.*

PLATE 135. *Mark of the printer Claudius Servianus, by an unknown master, Lyons,*
1550. Original size.

PLATE 136. *Escutcheon of the Counts Fugger-Kirchberg-Weissenhorn, probably by Bernard Salomon, from Jacob de Strada's* Epitome thesauri antiquitatum, *printed by Jean de Tournes, Lyons, 1553. ⅞ original size.*

PLATE 137. *Various decorative borders used by the print shops of Jean de Tournes and Anton Gryphius in Lyons, 1559–1569.* CENTER: *Printer's mark of Anton Gryphius, used as early as the 1530's by Anton's father Sebastian Gryphius. All 92% of original size.*

PLATE 138. ABOVE: *Mark of the printer Guillaume Roville, Lyons, 1563, probably by Bernard Salomon.* BELOW: *Mark occurring in books printed by Pierre Landry, Lyons, ca. 1583. Both 98% of original size.*

PLATE 139. *Decorative borders by Bernard Salomon, the top three used by the prin-ter Antoine Vincenti and the others by Guillaume Roville, both of Lyons, 1558–1562. All original size.*

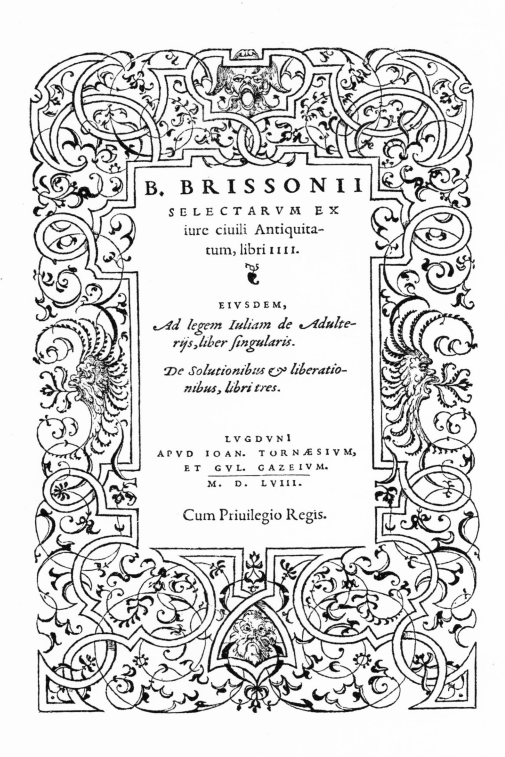

B. BRISSONII
SELECTARVM EX
iure ciuili Antiquita-
tum, libri IIII.

EIVSDEM,
Ad legem Iuliam de Adulte-
rijs, liber singularis.

De Solutionibus & liberatio-
nibus, libri tres.

LVGDVNI
APVD IOAN. TORNÆSIVM,
ET GVL. GAZEIVM.
M. D. LVIII.

Cum Priuilegio Regis.

PLATE 140. *Decorative border by Bernard Salomon, from the print shop of Jean de Tournes (and Guillaume Gazeau), Lyons, 1558. Original size.*

Nātiuam Aemylij Ferretti hîc icona cernis:
Muta quidem est icon, hęmylus ast is erat.

PLATE 141. *Portraits of the jurists Émile Ferretti and André Tiraquelle, presumably by Bernard Salomon, from works by these scholars printed in Lyons by Macé Bonhomme (1553) and Claude Senneton (1559), respectively. Original size.*

PLATE 142. *Ornaments, probably by Bernard Salomon, from the print shop of Jean de Tournes, Lyons, 1558. Original size.*

PLATE 143. *Initials by artists of the school of Bernard Salomon, from the print shop of Jean de Tournes, Lyons, 1575. Original size.*

PLATE 144. *Initials by artists of the school of Bernard Salomon, from the print shop of Jean de Tournes, Lyons, 1576. Original size.*

PLATE 145. *Initials by artists of the school of Bernard Salomon, from the print shop of Jean de Tournes, Lyons, 1559; also, the mark of the Parisian printer Michel Fezandat, 1547. All original size.*

PLATE 146. ABOVE LEFT: *Mark, probably by Bernard Salomon, of the printer to the royal court Jean de Tournes, Lyons.* ABOVE RIGHT: *Mark of the printer Scipio de Gabiano, Lyons, a contemporary of de Tournes.* BELOW LEFT: *Mark of the printer Pietro da Fino, Venice, 1568.* BELOW RIGHT: *Mark of the printer Charlotte Guillard, Paris.*

PLATE 147. *Alphabet by an unknown pupil of Bernard Salomon, from the print shop of Jean de Tournes, Lyons, 1576. Original size.*

PLATE 148. *Title page by the artist with the monogram G L, from the print shop of Sibylle de la Porte, Lyons, 1588 (design probably used earlier). Original size.*

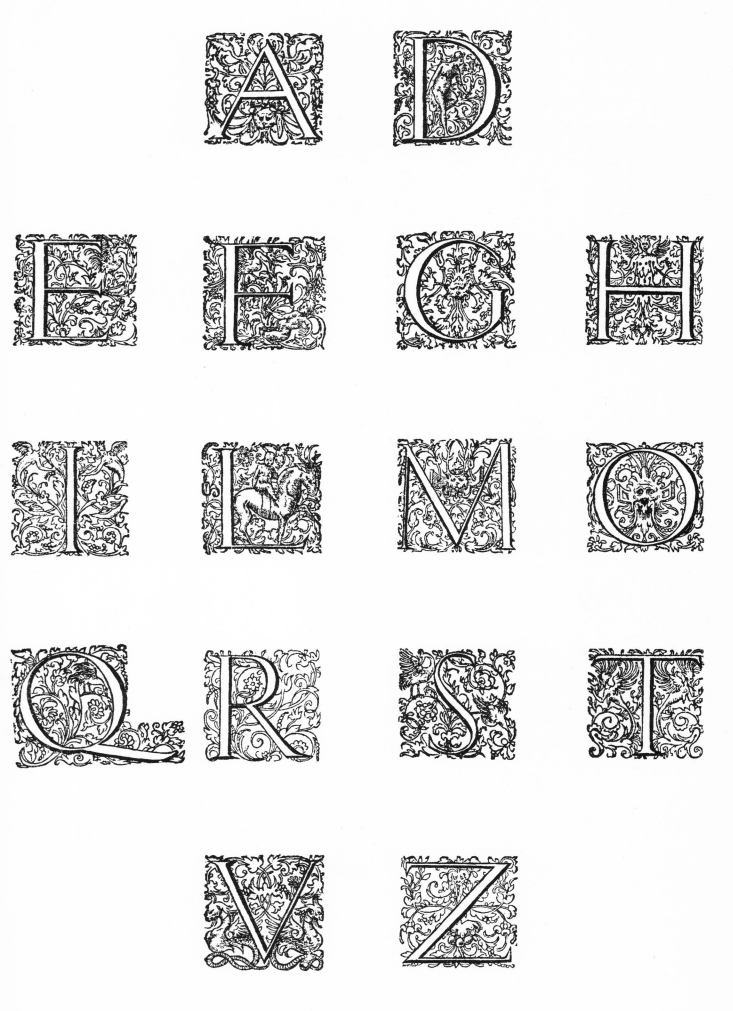

PLATE 149. *Alphabet by an unknown master, from the print shop of Macé Bon-homme, Lyons, 1566. Original size.*

PLATE 150. *Alphabet, probably by a pupil of Bernard Salomon, from the print shop of Guillaume Roville, Lyons, 1563. Original size.*

PLATE 151. *Initials and Plantin's mark, by an unknown master, from the print shop of Christophe Plantin, Antwerp, 1563. Original size.*

PLATE 152. *Initials from the print shop of Christophe Plantin, Antwerp, 1563. Original size. The E with the Three Kings and the O with King David are by Peter van der Borcht, the other letters by an unknown master.*

PLATE 153. *Initials by an unknown master, from the print shop of Christophe Plantin, Antwerp, 1563. Original size.*

PLATE 154. *Two emblems, probably by Hans Sebald Beham, for the print shop of Christian Egenolph, Frankfurt, 1546. Original size.*

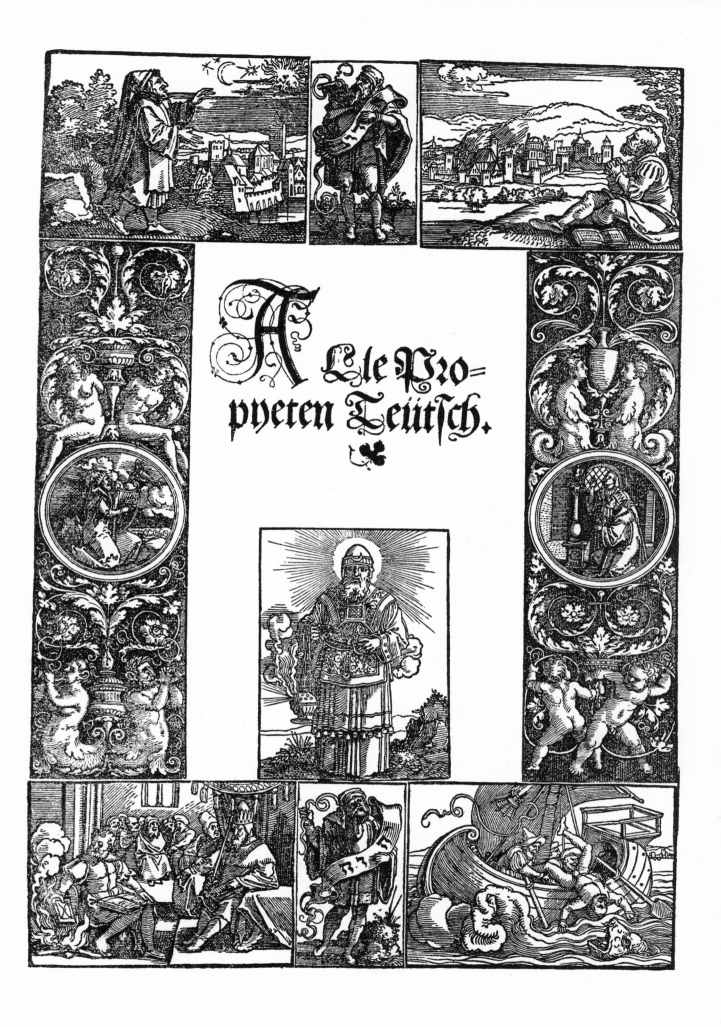

PLATE 155. *Decorated title page, the vertical panels by Hans Sebald Beham, from the print shop of Christian Egenolph, Frankfurt, 1536. Original size.*

PLATE 156. *Alphabet by the artist with the monogram* ⊞ *, from the print shop of Christian Egenolph, Frankfurt, ca. 1542. Original size.*

PLATE 157. *Title page by Virgil Solis, for a Lutheran Bible edition issued by Sigmund Feyerabend, Frankfurt, 1563. 94% of original size.*

PLATE 158. *Illustrations by Virgil Solis for Sigmund Feyerabend's 1563 Bible, Frankfurt. Original size.*

PLATE 159. *Illustrations by Virgil Solis for Sigmund Feyerabend's 1563 Bible, Frank-furt. Original size.*

PLATE 160. *Illustrations by Virgil Solis for Sigmund Feyerabend's 1563 Bible, Frankfurt. Original size.*

PLATE 161. *Illustration by Jost Amman, made for juridical works issued for the firm of Sigmund Feyerabend, Frankfurt, 1570. Also, tailpiece designed for Feyerabend by an unknown master. Both original size.*

PLATE 162. *Printer's marks by Jost Amman for Sigmund Feyerabend, Frankfurt.*
97% *of original size.*

PLATE 163. ABOVE: *Printer's mark by Jost Amman for Hieronymus Feyerabend,*
Frankfurt, 1567. BELOW: *Printer's mark by Tobias Stimmer for Sigmund Feyer-*
abend, Frankfurt, 1577. Both 97% of original size.

D. ANDREAE

TIRAQVELLI
REGII IN CV,
RIA PARISIENSI
Senatoris dignis-
simi,
OPERA OMNIA,

Quæ hactenus extant, Septem Tomis di-
stincta: quorum hic Primus
continet libros:
DE NOBILITATE ET IVRE
PRIMIGENIORVM.

Iam denuò recusa, & à plurimis mendis,
quibus antè scatebant, repurgata.
FRANCOFVRTI.
M. D. LXXIIII.

·SIGMVND· ·FEIRABENDT·

PLATE 164. *Title page of the Complete Works of the jurist André Tiraquelle,*
designed by Jost Amman, from the print shop of Sigmund Feyerabend, Frankfurt,
1574. Original size.

PLATE 165. *Escutcheon of Bishop Johann Egolph of Augsburg, drawn by Jost Amman, from the* Works of Tiraquelle *printed by Sigmund Feyerabend, Frankfurt, 1574. Original size.*

PLATE 166. *Portrait of Tiraquelle, from the edition of his works issued by Sigmund Feyerabend, Frankfurt, 1574; see Plates 141, 164 and 165. Original size.*

PLATE 167. *Initials designed by Jost Amman for print shops in Frankfurt, ca. 1567. Original size.*

PLATE 168. *Initials designed by Jost Amman for print shops in Frankfurt, ca. 1567. Original size.*

PLATE 169. *Initials designed by Jost Amman for print shops in Frankfurt, ca. 1567.*
Original size.

PLATE 170. *Title page (with scenes from Roman legendary history) by Jost Amman, for the Sigmund Feyerabend edition of Livy, Frankfurt, 1568. $\frac{7}{8}$ original size.*

PLATE 171. *Two printer's marks by Jost Amman, for the print shop of Sigmund Feyerabend, Frankfurt, 1568. Original size.*

IN STVDIO-
SORVM GRATIAM A.
MENDIS OMNIBVS
probè expurgatorum.

PARS SECVNDA.

M. D.   LXXII.

Francofurti ad
Mænum.

PLATE 172. *Title page and ornament by Jost Amman, from the print shop of Sigmund Feyerabend, Frankfurt, ca. 1572. Original size.*

PLATE 173. *Decorative borders by Jost Amman from the print shop of Sigmund Feyerabend, Frankfurt, ca. 1571. Original size.*

PLATE 174. ABOVE: *Decorative border, with scenes from Ovid's* Metamorphoses, *by Jost Amman.* BELOW: *Escutcheon of Canon Wolfgang Albert of Würzburg, also by Amman, from a book issued by Sigmund Feyerabend, Frankfurt, 1586. Both original size.*

PLATE 175. *Marks by Jost Amman for Sigmund Feyerabend, Frankfurt.* BELOW:
*For Feyerabend in collaboration with Johann Herbst (Oporinus) of Basle. Both
original size.*

DE ANTIQVITATIBVS

IVDAICIS LIBRI xx. QVIBVS IN FINE

LOCO APPENDICIS VITA IOSEPHI PER IPSVM
conscripta, est adiecta: De bello Iudaico Libri VII. ex collatione Græco-
rum Codicum accuratè castigati: Contra Apionem Libri II. pro corru-
ptißimis antea, iam ex Græco itidem non solum emendati, sed etiam sup-
pleti, ac integritati pristinæ restituti: De imperio rationis, siue de Mac-
chabæis Liber vnus, denuò recognitus; Antehac à Græca linguæ peritis-
simo, ac historiarum studiosißimo viro in Latinum sermonem trans-
lata, & ad exemplum Græci Codicis accuratè distincta.

NVNC VERO SVMMA CVM DILIGENTIA CHRONOLO-
gia ad caput vniuscuiusque folij, cum ex veterum tum recentiorum Scriptorum
Commentarijs, cumq; scholijs necessarijs, per doctum quendam virum in
communem Rei literariæ vtilitatem recens concinnata.

CVM FIGVRIS ET INDICE LOCVPLETISSIMO.

FRANCOFORTI.
CIↃ. IↃ IXXX.

PLATE 176. *Title page (with the Judgment of Solomon) by Jost Amman, from the print
shop of Sigmund Feyerabend, Frankfurt, 1580. Original size.*

PLATE 177. *Last mark of Sigmund Feyerabend designed by Jost Amman, probably in 1590 (the year of the Frankfurt publisher's death). Original size.*

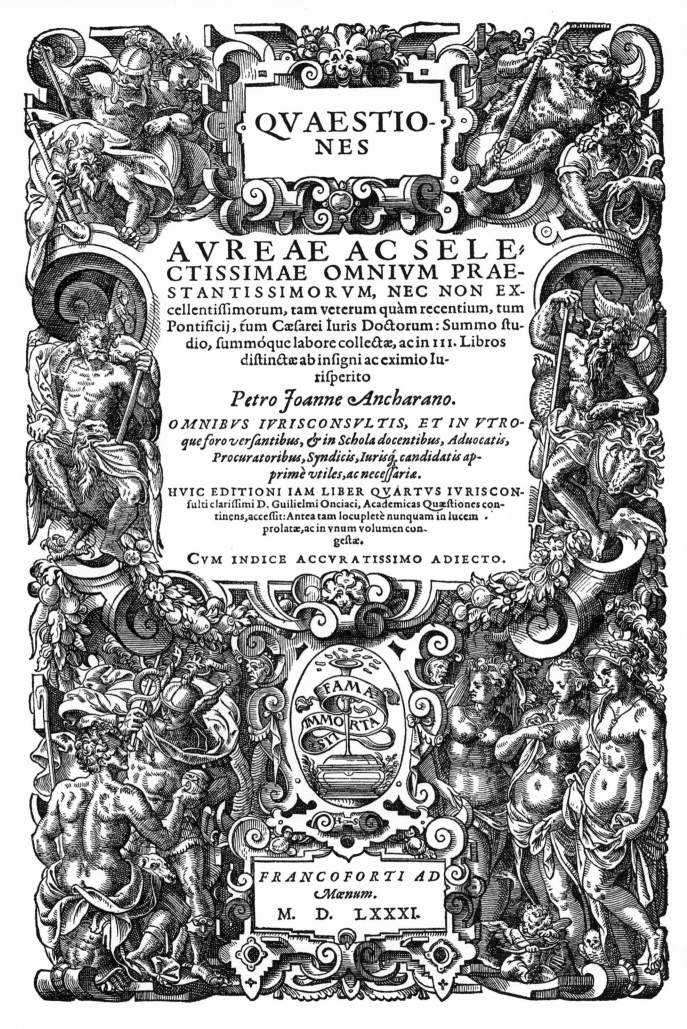

QUAESTIO-NES

AVREAE AC SELE-
CTISSIMAE OMNIVM PRAE-
STANTISSIMORVM, NEC NON EX-
cellentiſſimorum, tam veterum quàm recentium, tum
Pontificij, tum Cæſarei Iuris Doctorum: Summo ſtu-
dio, ſummóque labore collectæ, ac in III. Libros
diſtinctæ ab inſigni ac eximio Iu-
riſperito

Petro Joanne Ancharano.

OMNIBVS IVRISCONSVLTIS, ET IN VTRO-
que foro verſantibus, & in Schola docentibus, Aduocatis,
Procuratoribus, Syndicis, Iurisq́ candidatis ap-
primè vtiles, ac neceſſariæ.

HVIC EDITIONI IAM LIBER QVÀRTVS IVRISCON-
ſulti clariſſimi D. Guilielmi Onciaci, Academicas Quæſtiones con-
tinens, acceſſit: Antea tam locupletè nunquam in lucem
prolatæ, ac in vnum volumen con-
geſtæ.

CVM INDICE ACCVRATISSIMO ADIECTO.

FAMA IMMORTALIS

FRANCOFORTI AD
Mænum.
M. D. LXXXI.

PLATE 178. *Title page (with the Judgment of Paris), presumably by Jost Amman,*
from the print shop of Sigmund Feyerabend, Frankfurt, 1581. Original size.

Hoſtibus haud tergo, ſed forti pectore notus.

PLATE 179. ABOVE: *Printer's mark by an unknown master, from the shop of Crafft Miller, Strasbourg, 1537.* BELOW: *Mark by Jost Amman for the printer Sigmund Feyerabend, Frankfurt, when he was associated with Weigand Han and Georg Rab. Both 98% of original size.*

PLATE 180. ABOVE: *Printer's mark by Tobias Stimmer, from the print shop of Sigmund Feyerabend, Frankfurt, ca. 1574, 94% of original size.* BELOW: *Printer's mark by Jost Amman for Sigmund Feyerabend, Frankfurt, ca. 1590. 85% of original size.*

PLATE 181. *Printer's marks by Jost Amman for Sigmund Feyerabend, Frankfurt.*
ABOVE: *From 1587, when Feyerabend was associated with Heinrich Tack and*
Peter Fischer. BELOW: *From 1568, when Feyerabend was associated with Weigand*
Han's heirs and Georg Rab. Both original size.

PLATE 182. ABOVE LEFT: *Printer's mark by Jost Amman for Sigmund Feyerabend, Frankfurt, in association with Heinrich Tack and Peter Fischer, 1587.* ABOVE RIGHT: *Printer's mark for Feyerabend by Virgil Solis, 1565.* CENTER: *Printer's mark by Amman for Feyerabend.* BELOW, LEFT TO RIGHT: *Printer's mark for Andreas Gessner, Zurich, possibly by Christoph Schweitzer; mark of Arnold Birkmann, Cologne; mark for Feyerabend by Amman. All 86% of original size.*

PLATE 183. ABOVE: *Printer's mark by Jost Amman for Sigmund Feyerabend in association with Simon Hutter, Frankfurt, 1564, 94% of original size.* BELOW: *Printer's mark by Melchior Lorch (the Formschneyder was Lucas Maier) for Feyerabend, ca. 1577, 85% of original size.*

PLATE 184. ABOVE: *Illustrated genealogy by Jost Amman from the book* Coutumes
de Bourgogne, *published by Sigmund Feyerabend, Frankfurt, ca, 1574.* BELOW:
Tailpiece, probably by Virgil Solis. Both 98% of original size.

IN CRIMINALIBVS
CAVSIS.

A VARIIS QVI·
BVSQVE EXCELLENTIS-
SIMIS IVRECONSVLTIS, CONSCRIPTO-
rum: singulari verò studio, diligentia, labore & industria, Ioan. Baptistæ Ziletti, V. I. D. Veneti, recens in
hunc ordinem, secundum materiarum digni-
tatem, congestorum: sub Tomi
duplicis partitione.

TOMVS PRIMVS.
QVAE OMNIBVS IN IVRE, PRAESERTIM FORI
versantibus, quam necessaria & vtilia. Iam denuò ad eorum
communem vsum multò accuratiùs & elegantiùs,
quàm antea, typis tradita sunt.

Cum Summarijs, omniùmque ad Praxim necessariorum,
INDICE locupletissimo

FRANCOFORTI
AD MOENVM, 1577.

PLATE 185. *Title page by Jost Amman (Formschneyder Lucas Maier), from the print shop of Sigmund Feyerabend, Frankfurt, 1577. 96% of original size.*

PLATE 186. ABOVE: *Printer's mark (Fame with an eagle) by Jost Amman, from the shop of Sigmund Feyerabend, Frankfurt.* BELOW: *Mark by Tobias Stimmer, from the same shop. Both original size.*

PLATE 187. *Initials by Mathias Gerung, for a Missal from the print shop of Sebald Mayer, Dillingen (Germany), 1555. 71% of original size.*

PLATE 188. *Initials by an unknown master, from the print shop of Michael Zimmermann, Vienna, 1560's. 96% of original size.*

PLATE 189. *Initials by Michel Ostendorfer, from the print shop of Peter Apianus, Ingolstadt (Germany), ca. 1533. Original size.*

PLATE 190. *Title page designed and cut by Peter Hille, from the print shop of*
Michael Hentzken, Berlin, 1578. ¾ *original size.*

PLATE 191. *Alphabet by an unknown master, from the print shop of Hans Lufft,*
  Wittenberg, 1580. Original size.

PLATE 192. *Title page copied from a Johann von Calcar design by an unknown master, for the Anatomy of Andreas Vesalius, from the print shop of Johann Herbst (Oporinus), Basle, 1555. ¾ original size.*

PLATE 193. *The smaller initials by Johann von Calcar for the Vesalius issued by Johann Herbst, Basle, 1543. Original size.*

PLATE 194. *The five large initials from Vesalius editions of Johann Herbst, Basle.
I, O, Q, T are by Johann von Calcar and already appear in the edition of 1543.
The V, from the edition of 1555, is by an unknown master. All original size.*

PLATE 195. *Twelve of the small initials by an unknown master (copied after Johann von Calcar) from Johann Herbst's 1555 Basle edition of Galen. Original size.*

PLATE 196. *The other five small initials by an unknown master from Johann Herbst's
1555 Basle edition of Galen. Also, printer's mark of Johann Crato, Wittenberg,
1576. All original size.*

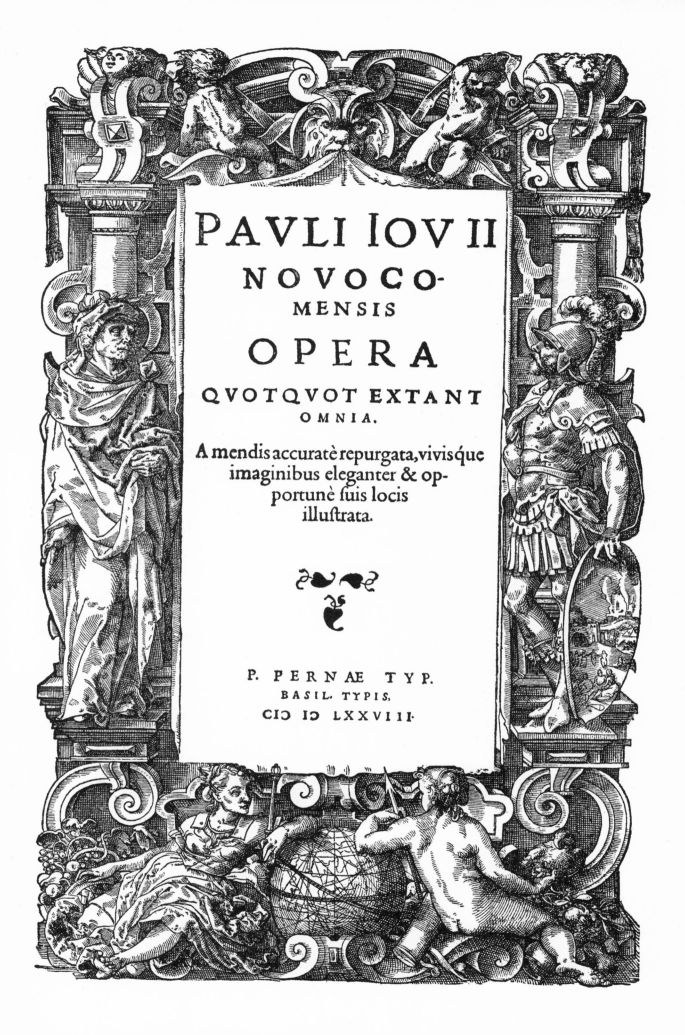

PAVLI IOVII
NOVO CO-
MENSIS
OPERA
QVOTQVOT EXTANT
OMNIA.

A mendis accuratè repurgata, vivisǿue
imaginibus eleganter & op-
portunè fuis locis
illuſtrata.

P. PERNAE TYP.
BASIL. TYPIS,
CIƆ IƆ LXXVIII.

PLATE 197. *Title page by Tobias Stimmer, from the print shop of Peter Perna, Basle,
1578.* $\frac{9}{10}$ *original size.*

PLATE 198. *Decorated page by Tobias Stimmer from the* Biblische Figuren *printed by Thomas Gwarin, Basle, 1576. Original size.*

PLATE 199. *Decorated page by Tobias Stimmer from the* Biblische Figuren *printed by Thomas Gwarin, Basle, 1576. Original size.*

PLATE 200. *Escutcheon of the Hartmann family of Eppingen, drawn by Tobias Stimmer, from a book issued by Thomas Gwarin, Basle, 1570. Original size.*

PLATE 201. *Escutcheon of Bernhard Wurmser of Scha[f]ftalsshaim, drawn by Tobias Stimmer, from a book issued by Thomas Gwarin, Basle, 1570. Original size.*

LVCERNA PEDI-
BVS MEIS VER-
BVM TVVM•

PLATE 202. *Alphabet of Children, large initials E and M, with scenes from the Old Testament, and the printer's mark of Peter Perna, Basle, 1580, all by Tobias Stimmer. All original size.*

PLATE 203. ABOVE: *Printer's mark by Jost Amman for Sigmund Feyerabend, Frankfurt.* BELOW LEFT: *Mark of the Cologne printer Arnold Birkmann.* BELOW RIGHT: *Mark by Johann von Essen, from the print shop of Gerwin Calenius and Johann Quentel's heirs, Cologne. All original size.*

PLATE 204. ABOVE LEFT: *Mark of the printer Paul Queck, Basle.* ABOVE RIGHT: *Mark of the printer Eusebius Episcopius, Basle.* BELOW LEFT: *Mark of the printer Nicolaus Episcopius, Basle (father of Eusebius Episcopius).* BOTTOM RIGHT: *Mark of Sebastian Henricpetri, by Tobias Stimmer, Basle, ca. 1576. All original size.*

PLATE 205. *Decorative borders from the 1562 Galen edition issued by the heirs of Johann Froben, Basle. Also, an initial from the print shop of Johann Berg and Valentin Neuber, Nuremberg, 1548. All original size.*

IMPERATORVM ROMA=
NORVM OMNIVM ORI
ENTALIVM ET OCCIDEN
TALIVM VERISSIMAE IMAGINES
EX ANTIQVIS NVMISMATIS QVAM
FIDELISSIME DELINEATAE.

ADDITA CVIVSQVE VITAE

DESCRIPTIONE EX
THESAVRO IACOBI STRADAE
ET PERBREVI ELOGIO VNIVSCV-
IVSQVE. CARMINE. QVOD QVASI
EPITOME EST HISTORIAE. AD
IVVANDAM MEMORIAM.

TIGVRI EX OFFICINA ANDREAE
GESNERI. ANNO
1559.

PLATE 206. *Title page, possibly by Christoph Schweitzer, from the print shop of Andreas Gessner, Zurich, 1559. ⅜ original size.*

PLATE 207. *Title page by Jost Amman for a book on horse care from the print shop of Michael Manger, Augsburg, 1576. Original size.*

PLATE 208. *Initials by Hans Sebald Beham, from the print shop of Johann Petreius, Nuremberg, 1529. Original size.*

PLATE 209. *Initials by Hans Sebald Beham, from the print shop of Johann Petreius, Nuremberg, 1529. Original size.*

PLATE 210. *Title page by Johann von Essen for a Catholic translation of the New Testament printed by Johann Quentel's heirs and Gerwin Calenius, Cologne, 1564.* ¾ *original size.*

PLATE 211. *Initials with Biblical scenes by the artist with the monogram* ℏ, *from the print shop of Gerwin Calenius and Johann Quentel's heirs, Cologne, 1560's and 1570's. Original size.*

PLATE 212. *Initials with Biblical scenes by the artist with the monogram ♄ , from the print shop of Gerwin Calenius and Johann Quentel's heirs, Cologne, 1560's and 1570's. Original size.*

PLATE 213. *Portrait of the botanist Hieronymus Bock by David Kandel, from the Latin edition of Bock's herbal issued by Wendelin Rihel, Strasbourg, 1551. Original size.*

PLATE 214. *Two printer's marks, probably by David Kandel, from the shop of Wendelin Rihel, Strasbourg, 1555. Also, ornaments from the print shop of Gabriel Giolito, Venice, ca. 1556. All original size.*

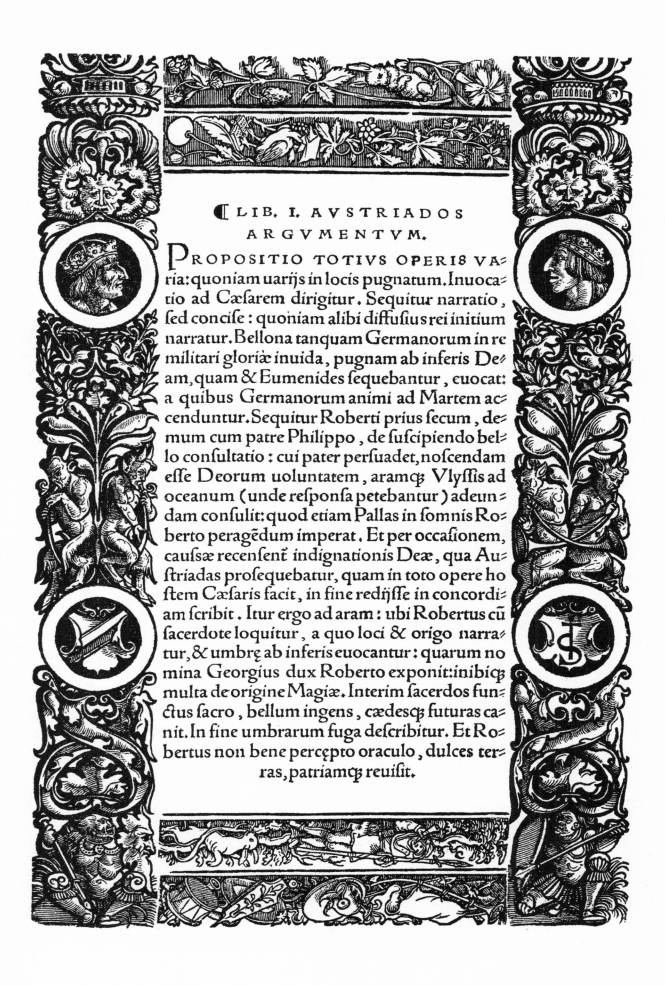

℀ LIB. I. AVSTRIADOS
ARGVMENTVM.

PROPOSITIO TOTIVS OPERIS VA=
ria: quoniam uarijs in locis pugnatum. Inuoca=
tio ad Cæsarem dirigitur. Sequitur narratio,
sed concise: quoniam alibi diffusius rei initium
narratur. Bellona tanquam Germanorum in re
militari gloriæ inuida, pugnam ab inferis De=
am, quam & Eumenides sequebantur, euocat:
a quibus Germanorum animi ad Martem ac=
cenduntur. Sequitur Roberti prius secum, de=
mum cum patre Philippo, de suscipiendo bel=
lo consultatio: cui pater persuadet, noscendam
esse Deorum uoluntatem, aramcʒ Vlyssis ad
oceanum (unde responsa petebantur) adeun=
dam consulit: quod etiam Pallas in somnis Ro=
berto peragēdum imperat. Et per occasionem,
caussæ recensēt indignationis Deæ, qua Au=
striadas prosequebatur, quam in toto opere ho
stem Cæsaris facit, in fine redijsse in concordi=
am scribit. Itur ergo ad aram: ubi Robertus cū
sacerdote loquitur, a quo loci & origo narra=
tur, & umbrę ab inferis euocantur: quarum no
mina Georgius dux Roberto exponit:inibicʒ
multa de origine Magiæ. Interim sacerdos fun=
ctus sacro, bellum ingens, cædescʒ futuras ca=
nit. In fine umbrarum fuga describitur. Et Ro=
bertus non bene percępto oraculo, dulces ter=
ras, patriamcʒ reuisit.

PLATE 215. *Decorated page by an unknown master from the book* De rebus gestis
Friderici I, *by Gunther Ligurinus, issued by Johann Schott, Strasbourg, 1531.*
The portraits are those of Emperor Maximilian II and Ferdinand, then King of
Hungary and Bohemia. Original size.

PLATE 216. *Title page, probably by Hans (Johannes) Nelt, from the print shop of Adam Berg, Munich, 1589.* ⅔ *original size.*

PLATE 217. *Portrait, in metal-cut, by a follower of Titian, of the scholar Francesco Alunno, from his* Fabrica del mondo, *published by Comin da Trino, Venice, 1556. Original size.*

PLATE 218. *Title page by a follower of Titian for a Latin translation of Galen issued by the heirs of Lucantonio Giunta, Venice, 1541. ¾ original size.*

I TRE LIBRI

PLATE 219. *Ornaments by an unknown master, from the print shop of Gabriel Giolito, Venice, 1555–1590. All original size.*

PLATE 220. *Portrait of the poet Lodovico Dolce from an edition of his Trasfor-mazioni issued by Gabriel Giolito, Venice, 1562. Original size.*

PLATE 221. ABOVE: *One of the marks used by Gabriel Giolito, Venice, 1556.* BELOW LEFT: *Mark from the print shop of Michele Tramezzino, Venice.* BELOW RIGHT: *Mark, attributed to Titian, from the print shop of Francesco Marcolini, Venice. All original size.*

PLATE 222. *Portrait of Dante from a Dante edition by the printer Giovanni Marchio Sessa, Venice, 1564. Original size.*

PLATE 223. *Part of an alphabet, with scenes from mythology and ancient history, from the print shop of Gabriel Giolito, Venice, second half of the sixteenth century. Original size.*

PLATE 224. *Initials from the print shop of Lorenzo Torrentino, Florence, 1550's, and vignette from the shop of Nicolaus Tridentinus, Venice, 1554. All original size.*

PLATE 225. *Initials from the print shop of Michele Tramezzino, Venice, 1549. Original size.*

PLATE 226. *Escutcheon of the Spaniard Juan Ortega de Carion of Burgos, who commissioned the Venetian printer Bartolomeo Zanetti to issue Mauro's* Sphaera *in 1537. Also, ornaments from the print shop of Gabriel Giolito, Venice, 1556.*

INDEXES

Index of Printers

Index of Artists

Index of Cities

INDEX OF PRINTERS

INDEX OF ARTISTS

INDEX OF CITIES